My Life with Tom Hughes

To Billye—
Hope this brings
back wonderful
memories!
Anne Hughes

My Life With

TOM HUGHES

A Personal Story of
The "Musicals Man" of Dallas

by

Anné Kouri Hughes
with
Janis Leibs Dworkis

TLH
PUBLISHERS

Dallas, Texas

Library of Congress Control Number: 2018910827
ISBN 978-1-5323-8724-1

TLH Publishers
Dallas, Texas

www.TheTomHughesProject.com

For our courageous children, Kenny, Ryan and Kyle—
who are brave enough to believe that their father travels with them always.

Foreword
by
Tommy Tune

I remember Tom Hughes as the legendary showman, tall and lean, elegantly dressed, cane in hand, striding onto the great stage of the Dallas Summer Musicals like Moses with his staff.

In front of the velvet curtain, spotlighted, before each and every performance, he welcomed the audience, informed us of the coming season, shared his specific insights about the evening's play and its stars, and then finished by thanking us for our presence.

Applause, applause, curtain up.

He had just exemplified what it takes to create and maintain a successful theatrical enterprise: He had given us his personal touch.

While at the University of Texas, I learned that the purpose of theatre is "to entertain and enlighten." Tom knew this and went about his life expressing these beliefs with passion and expertise. He was powerful. When he spoke, we listened. And the success of the Dallas Summer Musicals depended on, and thrived under, his direction. He had inherited a grand idea—home-grown seasons of great American musicals presented with savvy, panache, taste, and imagination. He paid that idea back with interest. His endeavors drew vast audiences throughout the great state and beyond. He gave generously and tirelessly.

We are very grateful. What a success!

With this book, Anné has given us the backstory we never really knew—the private man, husband, father, their grand romance—and in doing so, she has lovingly expanded the legend of this great Texas showman.

Ladies and gentlemen, the one and only—Tom Hughes.

Applause, applause, curtain up.

Tommy Tune
New York City
2018

Preface

Since April of 1994, it has been my heart's mission to keep their father's spirit present in the lives of our children.

Tom was a vibrant man, whose electrifying presence was felt each time he entered a room. Over the years, they have heard numerous stories about their father from me and countless others who were touched by Tom's kindness and humanity.

In keeping with that mission, I started this book project to preserve the many wonderful letters and photographs that tell further stories about Tom, his personal and public life, his contributions to the world of musical theatre and to the city of Dallas he loved so well.

I believe Tom would be delighted to see the vibrancy of the arts scene in his beloved city. I know he was honored to have been able to contribute to that.

But most importantly, I think he would be pleased to know that his kindness and support of others is still felt so keenly by the many people who have come forward and shared their stories with me over the years.

Anné Kouri Hughes
Dallas, Texas
2018

I had big plans for the evening of February 5, 1981—my friend Vivian and I were going to IHOP for a late-night coffee. It was opening night for North Texas State University's production of *Deathtrap*, and Vivian was working on the costume crew. Although we were both senior drama majors, I wasn't involved in the play.

So I came home from my dorm's intramural basketball practice, showered, threw on a pair of khaki slacks and a purple polo shirt, skipped the makeup, and went to pick her up.

"Anné, you won't believe what happened!" she said when I found her. "We've just been invited to the opening-night party! Can you believe it? Aren't you excited?"

"Excited? Are you crazy? Look at me."

This wasn't just any play. This was the annual Gaylord-Hughes production. Martha Gaylord, a well-known and beloved Dallas actress, and Tom Hughes, the producer and managing director of the Dallas Summer Musicals, had set up a scholarship for the University's drama department.

Martha Gaylord, Tom, George Wright (front row), Carol Weideman, and Wil Adams (back row) in the 1981 Gaylord-Hughes production of *Deathtrap*. I met Tom at the play's opening night party, February 5, 1981.

3

I was 21 years old the night I met Tom Hughes. A senior drama major, I attended North Texas State University in Denton.

Each year, they performed in a play alongside students to benefit the scholarship fund. It was a big draw, with crowds coming from Denton, Dallas, Fort Worth, and beyond. I'd heard those opening-night parties were very dressy affairs, catering to the patrons and trustees of the university.

"But this party will be different, really," Viv said. "There'll be people dressed in all kinds of things. You're fine just as you are. I promise. And some of our friends will be there, too."

I reluctantly agreed, and Viv ran off saying she'd be right back. She returned wearing a gorgeous black flowing top with spandex pants and heels.

"What are you doing?" I asked.

"I know—but it's the only thing I brought," she said. "I'll be wildly overdressed. Come on!"

I allowed myself to be dragged to the party, and as we approached the front walk of this gorgeous home, I felt a sense of impending doom. When the hostess opened the door, I saw beyond her to a small group of elegantly dressed theatre patrons, all in their tuxedos and floor-length cocktail dresses. I turned to Viv to save me, but she had flown across the room and was already at the piano with a group singing a rousing rendition of "What I Did for Love."

"May I help you?" the hostess asked.

"Yes, I hope so," I answered. "I'm so sorry, but there's been a terrible mistake. If I could just sit in your spare bedroom or dining room, I'll be fine waiting there for my friend."

"Of course not!" she said with a genuine, warm smile. And with that, she led me into the center of the gathering and tapped on the crystal goblet she was holding.

"Everyone! Everyone, I have an announcement!" she said. The room became quiet and the guests turned to look at their hostess. Standing next to her, I looked like the delivery girl—and they looked at me like I *was* the delivery girl.

"Everyone, one of our guests has brought a friend. I'd like to introduce you to . . ." She turned to me and quietly asked, "What is your name, dear?"

"Anné. Anné Kouri." I said it as quietly as I could without being completely rude.

"This is Anné. Let's all make her feel welcome."

After a silent but pronounced beat, the guests all turned back to their conversations.

"May I get you a drink, dear?" the hostess asked.

"Oh, no thank you. Really, I'll just wait for my friend."

"No, I insist. What can I bring you?"

I asked for a Coke. As she walked back toward me with the drink in a beautiful glass, I could tell she was trying her best to put me at ease in what was clearly an awkward situation. I thanked her as she handed me

One of Tom's favorite roles was Sidney Bruhl
in the 1981 Gaylord-Hughes production of *Deathtrap*.

Tom's publicity portrait, late 1970s, not long before we met.

the drink—and then I dropped it. I have no idea how it happened, but the glass, the ice, and the Coke just slipped right through my fingers and scattered over the beautiful pale blue carpet into the beautiful living room with all the beautiful people. Chaos—polite chaos—ensued.

Someone immediately started passing paper towels from the kitchen, and Viv and a few others helped me sop up the mess. Through my tears, I apologized, and the hostess assured me it was all right, everything would be fine. I had never been more embarrassed in my life.

At one point, I looked in the direction of the kitchen and met the kindest pair of eyes I had ever seen. It was Tom Hughes, looking at me with true compassion. I had seen him around campus from time to time, and everyone said he was quite prominent in theatre, but I didn't know much more than that. And now here he was, the source of our paper-towel brigade, grabbing rolls wherever he could find them.

Eventually the carpet was as dry as it was going to get that night, and the hostess asked if she could get me something else to drink. This time I asked for a vodka tonic—something completely clear, just in case. I spotted an overstuffed chair in the corner by the fireplace and decided to camp out there for the rest of the evening, nursing my drink and my wounded pride.

I was on my second vodka tonic when Mr. Hughes dragged a chair right up next to mine and sat down, something I later learned he rarely did at parties. He crossed his legs in a regal manner, leaned in toward me and said in a slow, conspiratorial tone, "You know, after the way you behaved at the Cannes Film Festival, I'm kind of surprised you have the nerve to show up here."

I looked him straight in the eyes and did not miss a beat.

"After the way I behaved? As I recall, *you* were the one who embarrassed us in front of the Countess!"

He looked at me and replied, "How was I to know she had a gun?"

And that was that.

Tom and I laughed and spoke non-stop for the remainder of the evening, just the two of us. We didn't talk about anything special—the show, the university, what I planned to do after college—but I could have stared into those eyes and talked with him forever. Then suddenly it was two o'clock in the morning, and we were the only ones still chatting away. Everyone except Viv had left, and she was almost asleep on the sofa. It was time to go.

What a magical night. I knew I would never forget it for as long as I lived. I thought, "What a delightful man. I believe he's the most interesting man my parents' age I've ever met."

That's exactly how I thought about Tom that night—as a wonderful gentleman of my parents' generation. After all, he was 49 years old. I was 21.

By the night we met, Tom had been producer and managing director of the Dallas Summer Musicals for twenty years—almost my entire life. But he had been in love with absolutely everything about theatre for as long as he could remember.

Lloyd Thomas Hughes, Jr. was born in 1931 and grew up on a cotton farm in Denton County. He began staging shows in his Carrollton backyard at the age of 4. At age 6, he performed a poem called "Poor Little Fly on the Wall" on *The Major Bowes Amateur Hour*,

Tom began "producing" shows in his Carrollton, Texas backyard at age 4.

At age 10, Tom was riding the streetcar by himself to see the summer productions at the Fair Park Band Shell.

Tom (far right) in his first leadership role, the first-grade band conductor, 1937. Tom often said with a smile, "I failed the cymbals. I failed the sticks. I failed the tambourine. They had no choice but to make me the conductor!"

a national radio talent show that would eventually become *The Ted Mack Amateur Hour* on television.

That same year, he gave another public performance as part of his grammar school elocution lessons. It was a poem called "Casablanca," a horribly depressing story about a boy who perished in a fire on an eighteenth-century battleship. I feel sure Tom chose that poem for the sheer drama of it. And I'm equally sure he gave a stunning performance. He was a successful student all the way through school.

Tom's father was in the Army and a merchant—and mostly absent throughout Tom's childhood. His mother, Kathryn Bond Hughes, was a kind and nurturing woman with whom Tom always had a wonderful relationship. As a grown man, he referred to his mother as "Lady Kathryn" when speaking to family and friends, an appropriate term given the respect and admiration he always felt for her.

Kathryn seemed to know just the right balance between nurturing her son and giving him the independence he needed. In fact, one hot summer evening in 1941, she allowed 9-year-old Tom to ride a street car across town by himself to see *Blossom Time* at the Fair Park Band Shell. This was the first performance of Opera Under the Stars, co-produced by the State Fair of Texas and Broadway mogul J.J. Shubert, and Tom didn't want to miss it.

That inaugural performance was a milestone for Dallas, although few could have imagined it at the time. Opera Under the Stars would eventually become the world-class Dallas Summer Musicals, the second-oldest musical theatre program in the country, still going strong today more than seventy-five years later.

For Tom—the handsome young boy in the thirty-cent seat sitting focused and enthralled—the evening was a turning point in his life, a night he would always remember. This was the night he knew he would pursue a life in theatre. It wasn't much of a decision or even a choice. It was simply a realization: This is who I am. And from *Blossom Time* on, Tom Hughes never wavered.

Tom attended every performance he possibly could that summer. The following year, the season was cancelled due to World War II. But in 1943, musical theatre was back—this time under the name Starlight Operettas—and so was 11-year-old Tom.

Knowing Tom, I suspect he was so excited, so engrossed, he probably wasn't even bothered by the discomfort of the Band Shell. The concrete amphitheatre held onto the heat of the day, and Dallas nights never cooled off very much anyway. Newspapers reported that audience members were constantly fanning themselves, swatting bugs, and straining to hear music and dialogue over aircraft noise, ambulance sirens, and even bullfrog calls from the nearby lagoon. An article in *The*

Dallas Morning News, August 26, 1947, noted: "More than once, a tender lovers' duet was interrupted by a shout of 'Bingo!'" from the State Fair Midway.

But to Tom, the place was magic. That hot, uncomfortable Band Shell was the only place he really wanted to be. As soon as he was old enough, he took a job selling soft drinks and seat cushions to the other patrons. His career in theatre had begun.

When Tom was 14, he approached his principal at Carrollton High School about putting on a play. Tom explained he didn't think it was fair for the school's play to be only for seniors. He wanted to produce one himself, as a freshman.

"Tommy, you know we don't have a drama department and we don't have additional funds for anything like that," the principal told him. "But if you're willing to do all the work and put it all together yourself, you can perform the play in our building."

Tom heard a resounding "yes!"

He immediately borrowed $100 from his mother and rounded up some friends to perform. Since he couldn't find any boys who were interested, he chose an all-girl play and then auditioned, rehearsed, and directed the actors. When *Nine Girls* premiered on February 28, 1946, it was immediately crowned a success. Not only did Tom make enough money from donations to pay his mother back, but, by popular demand, the play was performed for the entire student body the very next day.

It was Tom Hughes' first production.

Tom entered North Texas State College (now University of North Texas) to major in drama after graduating from high school at age 16. In college, he became convinced his talents were in producing, not acting. As a student, he produced and directed Varsity Club shows

Tom's first production was *Nine Girls* at Carrollton High School. He was a freshman. The cost of the play's scheduled one-night run was $100, which he borrowed from his mother. A second performance was held by popular demand.

and the Spring Musical Festival—while also becoming a top debater and serving as student body vice president, president of the student senate, assistant debate coach, and, as Tom described it, "a member of almost anything they'd let me in."

During summers, Tom continued to work at the Band Shell selling sodas and seat cushions and watching most every performance. It was during one of those outdoor performances in 1949—the final perfor-

mance of *Bloomer Girl*, starring Nanette Fabray—that an incident put Dallas musical theatre on the international map.

Miss Fabray had not been too keen on coming to Dallas. Given her mortal fear of bugs stemming from a childhood attack by a swarm of locusts in the Midwest, she had never performed outdoors. To quell her fears, management had assigned an assistant stage manager to spray her costume with insecticide each evening.

The way Tom told it, all had gone well until a cricket hit Miss Fabray in the face while she was singing. As the insect fell straight down into her costume and began to crawl around, Miss Fabray's high note went higher and higher until it became a piercing scream. In his confusion, the sound engineer turned the amplifiers up instead of down, and the note carried for blocks. Paralyzed with fear, Miss Fabray just kept screaming until the stage manager ran onto the stage and physically carried her off.

The "bug in the bosom" story was reported around the world that week in *The New York Times*, *Tokyo Times*, and *Newsweek*, among many other publications. Everyone was reading about musical theatre in Dallas, Texas.

In 1951, Tom graduated college, earning a bachelor's degree with honors in drama. He taught speech for one year at Michigan State University while completing his master's degree. The following year, in the middle of the Korean War, Tom enlisted in the U.S. Army.

After basic training, the Army placed Tom in its Intelligence Division at Camp Zama, Japan, southwest of Tokyo. In his second year of service, Tom was asked by General Maxwell Taylor to put some shows together to entertain the officers.

General Taylor was a well-respected officer who would later become Chairman of the Joint Chiefs of Staff under President John F. Kennedy. Tom was honored by the request and thrilled to be able to use his skills to serve the Army.

Tom enlisted in the Army in 1952 and was stationed in the Intelligence Division at Camp Zama, Japan.

Tom became producer and director of the Zama Players. His first production, *The Moon is Blue*, was such a success that most of the leisure-time funds went to theatre productions from that point forward. Before leaving the Army in 1955, Tom also produced *Cyrano de Bergerac*—one of his favorites, in which he also starred—and *The Play's the Thing*.

While in the Army, Tom produced *Cyrano de Bergerac*, one of his personal favorites. He starred in the Zama Players production, shown in rehearsal (above) and in performance (below).

Just before he left the Army and returned to Dallas,
Tom produced and starred in *The Play's The Thing*, August 1955.

Arriving back in Dallas, Tom sought career advice from longtime family friend, Dallas businessman and philanthropist Julius Schepps. That's when he learned Charles R. Meeker, Jr., managing director of State Fair Musicals, was looking for an assistant. Julius picked up the phone to make the connection for Tom, who was hired immediately.

Tom was soon promoted to house manager in the newly air-conditioned State Fair Music Hall. He assumed responsibility for ticket sales, the box office, seating the audience, managing the ushers, and cleaning the auditorium at the end of the night.

It was a pivotal moment in Tom's life, launching him into the career he had dreamed about. In 1964, Tom described it this way in a letter to Julius:

> *Those sergeant's stripes and fond memories of the Far East have pretty well faded into a dim but pleasant remembrance, and my memories now begin with that fateful day in your office, when you called a stranger to me by the name of C. R. Meeker, and started the chain of events responsible for the past nine years.*

Julius Schepps continued to mentor Tom until Julius' death in 1971. They met in person when their schedules allowed, and Tom sent him annual year-end letters to describe the Musicals' successes and failures, as well as his own personal growth. Tom's humility shone through in those letters—as did his dedication to his job and city, and gratitude to Julius—as in these examples from 1962-64:

> *I think perhaps the greatest strength a man can possess in his lifetime is to be able to know that he has a counsellor and an advisor, but most of all, a friend, never farther away than the phone. I have been blessed with this from you since my early youth and consider it my most treasured possession.*

> *As I look back on the departing year, I know full well that not all has been a success and that there have been mistakes on my part. Mistakes in judgement cannot and should not be excused, but my hope is that I do recognize them, profit from them, and try my best to see that they are not repeated.*

> *With your continued moral support and encouragement, I shall ever strive to move my steps in a direction that serves the Fair, the Musicals and the City.*

Dallas businessman and civic leader Julius Schepps (r.) with Dallas mayor R.L. Thornton. Julius was a longtime friend of Tom's family, and helped connect Tom to a career in theatre when Tom returned from the Army.

Tom, Hyman Charninsky, Charlie Meeker, and David Blackburn, members of the State Fair Musicals staff, 1950s.

Charlie Meeker, managing director and producer; Toni Beck, choreographer; and Tom, assistant managing director and producer; late 1950s.

The State Fair Music Hall, 1950s.

Tom's mother, Kathryn Bond Hughes, Tom, his aunt Bess Bond, and Tom's cousin Walter Bond, 1950s. Tom and Walter grew up spending summers together at their grandparents' home in Red Oak, Texas.

While Tom was settling into his new job as Charlie Meeker's assistant in the early 1950s, Philip S. Kouri was becoming a well-known attorney in Wichita Falls, Texas, about 150 miles away. Philip was also a man who loved to entertain. And as he was planning one particular party in 1956, a friend of his mentioned her daughter would be home from college that night.

"Of course, bring your daughter, too," Philip told his friend. It was an invitation that would change his life.

The moment Philip Kouri laid eyes on Beverly Barker, he fell in love. Although they'd never previously met, he introduced her to his friends that night as his future bride.

For her part, Beverly laughed at the silliness and went back to her drama studies at North Texas State College in Denton. She didn't give Philip another thought—until an engagement ring arrived in the mail four days later. She returned it immediately. He sent it right back.

Philip Kouri and Beverly Barker were married four months later. Exactly nine months and one week after their wedding date, my brother Kenny was born. I arrived two years later.

I grew up in a warm and joyful home filled with reverence for the arts, philosophy, theatre, and literature, the love of a large extended family—and alcoholism. When my father was present and sober, no family could have been more wonderful. He was a "seasonal drinker" and could be sober for months at a time. When he was on a binge, however, life at home was frightening. My loving and warm extended family—Granny, Aunt Leta, and Uncle Ellis—would often step in to help care for us.

My older brother Kenny, 13, and I, 11, were always together. With his gregarious personality, everyone loved being around him, especially me. Only one year apart in school, we attended the same high school and college.

My mother addressed the situation head on. She told us my father had a disease. Just like some people have cancer, your father has alcoholism, she would say, and you wouldn't stop loving or respecting a parent with cancer. My mother would not tolerate any disrespect toward our father from Kenny or me. But neither did she gloss over his behavior and pretend all was normal.

Although my mother tried to shield us from my father's drunken outbursts, Kenny was my true protector. He was my hero. He would pull me to hide under the bed with him or help me run out of the house in our pajamas when we needed to. I absolutely adored and trusted him.

If Kenny wanted to play football or basketball, I played football or basketball. If he wanted to play Rock 'em Sock 'em Robots, I was right there with him. I always wanted to be near my brother. And I was.

My parents, Beverly and Philip Kouri in 1956, leaving for their honeymoon. They lived in Wichita Falls, Texas, where my mother was involved in community theatre, and my father was an attorney. They were both active in the local arts community throughout their lives.

While I was growing up in Wichita Falls, Tom was busy bringing world-class theatre to the city he loved. With his promotion to assistant managing director and producer, Tom was truly in his element. More than any other aspect of theatre, Tom loved producing shows, building them from scratch—choosing the play and the cast, overseeing the sets, the costumes, music, rehearsals, all of it. He loved pulling together the thousands of details that would have driven most people mad, and then watching the magic happen when the curtain opened. Tom produced shows throughout his entire career. He also presented national touring shows that had been produced in New York and elsewhere.

Whether Tom was producing or presenting a show, he was always there for anyone who performed at his Music Hall. He was physically present for every performance and stayed to the end, even accompanying actors to the stage door when they signed autographs and met audience members. The way Tom saw it, the Music Hall was his house, and the staff, actors, and audience were his guests.

Many actors have commented through the years how much they appreciated knowing Tom was always on-site, his steady presence ready for any last-minute emergency requests—such as Marlene Dietrich's rather unusual request in 1960.

The internationally acclaimed cabaret singer was in town to star in her own show, *The Marlene Dietrich Show*, accompanied by Burt Bacharach. Tom described Miss Dietrich as one of the most glamorous women in the world. He wanted to make sure everything was perfect for her performance, so he set a quick-change room for her, stage left.

Just before the opening night performance, Tom took a call on the house phone saying Miss Dietrich needed a scrub brush and a pail of soapy water. He told her he'd be right there.

"Ma'am, what do you need?" he asked when he arrived backstage.

"I need my quick-change room scrubbed," she said. Tom told her he would send someone right back to do it.

"No, Tom. I'll do it," she told him.

"No, *I'll* do it," Tom said.

"No, I'd rather do it," she told him. "I'll do it right."

Every year, Tom went to New York and Los Angeles to audition actors for the leads and principal roles in the upcoming season. It was an exciting time for him and the staff who accompanied him, but a pressure cooker as well. The decisions they made during those scouting trips would affect both the short-term and long-term health of the Musicals. Would audiences respond well to this or that actor? Would the quality of this summer's performances encourage audiences to return next year, or possibly even become season-ticket subscribers?

In addition to the New York and Los Angeles trips, hundreds of hopefuls would come to the Music Hall each April to audition for that season's chorus. Tom said many times that out of every 500 people he saw, he wanted to hire 490. But he could only choose sixteen each year: eight boys and eight girls, the best

Tom Poston, Ruth Collins Sharp, Charles Sharp, Shirley Jones, Tom, and Jack Cassidy, 1959. Shirley and Jack were in town starring in *Wish You Were Here*. Charles was a Dallas Summer Musicals board member who became president and chairman of the board in 1963. Ruth was one of the founding members of the Dallas Summer Musicals Guild and a board member. Upon Charles' death in 1984, she became honorary chairman of the board until her death in 2017.

Tom, seated, with Gordon Wynne, Jr., a production manager for the State Fair Musicals in the 1950s. Gordon toured with Judy Garland as her production manager throughout Europe and the U.S., including a Command Performance for the Queen of England. He went on to become an award-winning television and Broadway producer.

Winner of Academy, Tony, and Golden Globe Awards, Judy Garland played to sold-out houses when the national tour of *The Judy Garland Show* came to the Music Hall, 1957. Age 35 at the time, she had already been singing, dancing, and acting for more than thirty years.

singers and dancers he could find. Not only would those sixteen performers be cast in the Dallas Summer Musicals season, but they would also earn their membership in the Actors' Equity Association—the golden ticket to audition for Broadway shows. Every single person who auditioned wanted "in."

In 1958, Tom held Dallas auditions for specific roles, as well as the chorus, in that summer's *The King and I*.

Up on stage among the adult singers and dancers was an energetic and highly talented 12-year-old girl. Tom's mother was in the audience that day, and she pulled Tom aside.

"Tom, are you noticing that little blonde up there?" she asked, pointing.

"Yes, Mother," he said with a sigh. "We are well aware of Sandy."

Sandy Duncan had come with her mother from Tyler to audition for the children's roles. But she was so enthusiastic and excited, that when Tom called the adults forward by groups, she jumped right in. Even among the adults, she was a standout. Tom was thrilled to cast her in the production.

In 1960, Tom had the opportunity to jumpstart another show-business career. During the seasonal chorus auditions, one 20-year-old college student from Houston stood out in every way. At 6'6", he was not only a head taller than everyone else, but he was one of the most talented dancers Tom had ever seen. He immediately hired the young man for the upcoming season, casting him in *West Side Story* and *Redhead*.

His name was Tommy Tune.

When Charlie Meeker left to pursue a career with Six Flags over Texas on January 1, 1961, Tom became managing director and producer of the State Fair Musicals. At age 29, he was certainly young to take on such responsibility.

But as he always said, this was the job for which he'd been born. He was ready, up to the task, and eager to get started.

Tom realized one of his most immediate tasks was to establish much-needed ongoing community support.

He asked six prominent women—including Margaret Golden, Carolyn Lupton, and Ruth Collins Sharp—to join him for lunch at the Cipango Club to discuss what form that support might take. By the time dessert was finished, the Dallas Summer Musicals Guild was born.

An all-volunteer organization, the Guild is still going strong today more than sixty years later. Guild members contribute to the Musicals financially, as well as host opening-night cast parties and weekend buffets. In return for their service, members enjoy a variety of social opportunities to meet and interact with cast members. It's a perfect match for theatregoers who love to give back to their community.

It was through the Guild that Tom established his life-long friendship with Ruth and Charles Sharp. Charles became president and chairman of the board in 1963. He was a wonderful mentor to Tom until his death in 1984, at which time Ruth became honorary board chair. Tom and Ruth were extremely close for the remainder of Tom's life.

Tom presenting flowers to Carol Channing at Love Field in 1960, upon her arrival
for that summer's performances of *An Evening with Carol Channing*.

The 1961 season had been planned before Tom took over, and he couldn't change the line-up. While he knew the coming season needed to be a money-maker since the Musicals had lost money the previous few years, he wasn't too worried. After all, the season included *Billion Dollar Baby*, planned as a major revival headed for Broadway. Tom was hopeful it would put the Musicals in the black.

Instead, the show was a total disaster, labeled by Tom as the "all-time worst production" in the Musicals' history.

Tom always knew his audiences were the ultimate arbiters of his work; his own opinions, and even those of the critics, were secondary. More than once, he explained to the public and to journalists that it just wasn't possible to fully predict a city's response to a show. There were solid shows from which he expected good reviews but not much more—and yet they turned out to be rousing successes. There were others that unexpectedly sank without much enthusiasm. But *Billion Dollar Baby* was in a class all by itself, described by one newspaper as "almost a death blow" to the Musicals.

In fact, when the season ended, the board of directors talked about closing the Musicals and cutting their losses. But before making the final decision, they gave Tom the opportunity to speak to the board. Not surprisingly, he made an impassioned plea to keep the Musicals going and to give him an opportunity to turn it around.

Tom was persuasive and the board agreed, but with one significant caveat: They would keep the Musicals open for one more season if Tom could raise $100,000 for expenses that fall—*before* the next season. It was a chance, and Tom took it.

With the help of generous benefactors, he did raise the money. The Musicals stayed alive through the winter of 1961-62, giving Tom the opportunity to produce his own first season for the following summer. In a January 2, 1962 letter to Julius Schepps, Tom wrote:

It would not be possible for me to express in words the great appreciation I feel for your assistance in keeping the Musicals alive, or at least giving us a chance to live and continue to grow. I'm certain that without your strength and counsel in the meeting that the New Year would look dark indeed. For this I am forever grateful.

It is a good feeling to start the New Year with an opportunity, and with the greatest personal challenge ever presented me. I thought that last year on this date I had been given my greatest challenge and opportunity. Perhaps this was true, and growth as a person is only achieved when the opportunities and challenges continue to present themselves year in and year out.

Thank you once again for your advice and counsel during the past year, and for your belief in the Musicals and your faith in me. I shall do my utmost in the New Year to live up to the opportunity which you have helped to make possible.

When it came to planning that 1962 make-it-or-break-it season, Tom knew just what he wanted—the kind of star power no one could resist. He turned to Julie Andrews and Carol Burnett, whose two-woman show, *Julie and Carol at Carnegie Hall*, had been a smashing success. His first order of business was to sign them, which he did right away. Then Julie Andrews became pregnant—and immediately cancelled.

Tom's first publicity portrait. He had just been named producer and managing director, 1961.

Tom, June Walker, Pat Remick, Toni Beck, James Stewart, Gus Schirmer, James Leon, and Ira Bloom at Nola Studios in New York, during the spring casting session for the Dallas Summer Musicals, 1961 season. This was Tom's first season as managing director and producer.

Production meeting in 1961 with music director James Leon, Tom,
director Gus Schirmer, production manager H.R. Poindexter, and choreographer Toni Beck.

If you'll sit, we'll play. Take off your coats, loosen your girdles, remember the old days of outdoors when it was 104, 105 degrees, and stay with us. You can get a refund at the end of the show—but we'll play for you.

And most of them stayed.

—Tom Hughes, 1962

after acknowledging to the audience that the air-conditioning went out on the season's opening night. This became the first of his curtain speeches. Tom spoke to his audience more than 1,500 times over the course of his career.

Tom tried to talk Carol Burnett into keeping the commitment and doing a one-woman show, but as many times as he asked, she refused. Finally, he flew to New York and started visiting her agent's office every day, practically camping out, as he put it. Eventually, she agreed. Tom used to say she had no choice—because if she didn't, she'd find a grown man crying on her doorstep every morning when she went out to bring in the milk.

The State Fair Musicals separated from the State Fair of Texas that year and become an independent organization known as the Dallas Summer Musicals, Inc. At the helm of this newly minted organization, after years of learning from Charlie Meeker, and with the future of the Musicals resting on his shoulders, Tom might have been a bit nervous. But he had worked hard and was confident and excited to produce his own shows for the people of Dallas: *Wildcat, Carousel, Carol Burnett in Person, Gypsy, The Merry Widow,* and *South Pacific.*

And then the air conditioning went out on the season's opening night.

It had broken down that afternoon, and there was just no way to fix it before curtain. So, as actress Peggy Cass got ready to step out on the stage for *Wildcat,* audience members were squirming and complaining.

Tom knew that a Dallas summer evening indoors without air conditioning was a dismal prospect—much worse than the Band Shell, where at least they had the occasional breeze. So, typical of Tom, he decided to face the issue head on. As someone held the curtain for him, he walked out on stage right and into the spotlight to speak directly to the audience.

"Good evening, everyone." He acknowledged the air-conditioning problem and then added, "If you'll

sit, we'll play. Take off your coats, loosen your girdles, remember the old days of outdoors when it was 104, 105 degrees, and stay with us. You can get a refund at the end of the show—but we'll play for you." Tom always said that if you tell the audience the truth, they'll generally stay with you. Most of them did stay that night.

That unplanned speech became the first of Tom's curtain speeches, a signature part of the evening for anyone who attended the Musicals. Tom would come out from stage right and speak directly to the audience, sharing something about the show, the story, the cast, the upcoming season, and letting the audience see just how excited he was about Dallas Summer Musicals.

Between that now-infamous and very warm night in 1962 and Tom's last season more than thirty years later, he spoke to his audience about 1,500 times—and they loved him for it. It was through these curtain talks that Tom became the face of Dallas Summer Musicals, and hundreds of thousands of audience members throughout the years felt they knew him personally. No matter what year it was, whether the show was a classic or brand new, whether the lead was a familiar actor or an exciting new talent, Tom was always there to connect the audience to the show. He absolutely loved those talks—his chance to share his passion for theatre with a few thousand of his closest friends.

The 1962 season was a stunning financial success, which Tom attributed completely to Carol Burnett. *Carol Burnett in Person* broke all existing records with 58,000 tickets sold. Tom credited her with bringing a level of excitement and star power to Dallas Summer Musicals that reinvigorated the entire organization.

"What happened in 1962 was simple. Carol Burnett made her first appearance on our stage. I have often said, in numerous appearances, that Carol saved the theatre. She was the real revitalizing force. She brought the magic back for us. She brought our audiences back to us," Tom said.

Another of Tom's favorite shows from that period was 1964's *Little Me*, starring Donald O'Connor. Tom said Donald's timing was impeccable, the dancers had never been better, the costumes and scenery—everything was exactly right.

"Imagine the coup of having Donald O'Connor do his first book musical comedy and to see that timing," he was quoted as saying.

"There's an electricity that takes off sometimes. Oh, it was a son-of-a-gun of a show. And Donald just couldn't have approached it with more dignity and talent, to where the excitement was just. . . it bubbled. Sometimes they [the audience] don't even remember the title, but they talk about that kind of magic. And if you think an audience is feeling that, how do you think I'm feeling?"

How was Tom feeling? It's pretty safe to say he was elated.

Throughout the 1960s, Tom increased the financial stability of Dallas Summer Musicals, brought new people in as subscribers, and exposed the city to the greatest works of musical theatre.

He brought Jack Benny, Milton Berle, Douglas Fairbanks, Jr., Robert Goulet, Harvey Korman, Juliet Prowse, John Raitt, Chita Rivera, and so many others to Dallas.

Carol Burnett returned twice in the 1960s—in *Calamity Jane* in 1963 and in 1967 with Jim Nabors in *Carol and Jim at the Music Hall*, which became the Musicals' second-best box office, just behind her 1962 performance.

Tom working with Tony Award winner Lawrence Kasha, who directed several shows for the Dallas Summer Musicals, 1963.

And in 1965, Tom decided it was time to share some of the Dallas Summer Musicals magic with the rest of the world—that magic being Sandy Duncan.

Margaret Rodgers, the Musicals coproducer, and Tom took 19-year-old Sandy to New York, hoping to help her find her first job outside North Texas.

Knowing her tremendous talent, they believed she could be successful nationally if the right people could just see her.

Tom and Margaret arranged all the trip details—flights, hotels, and auditions—and took her everywhere she needed to go. Sandy received not one, but four job offers that week, and has credited that trip with jumpstarting her career.

"I couldn't have had a career without Tom Hughes," Sandy has said. "I just wouldn't."

Carol Burnett and chorus rehearsing "I Don't Want to be Nelson Anymore" for the 1962 production *Carol Burnett in Person*.

What happened in 1962 was simple. Carol Burnett made her first appearance on our stage. I have often said that Carol saved the theatre. She was the real revitalizing force. She brought the magic back for us. She brought our audiences back to us.

—Tom Hughes

Comedians Marty Allen and Steve Rossi with Carol Burnett, *Carol Burnett in Person*, 1962.

Tom with coproducer Margaret Rodgers, director John Bishop, and music director Jack Lee, working on the Dallas Summer Musicals 1964 season.

Eddie Albert starring as Harold Hill in *The Music Man*, 1963, a role he performed on Broadway 1959-60.

Imagine the coup of having Donald O'Connor do his first book musical comedy and to see that timing. Oh, it was a son-of-a-gun of a show. And Donald just couldn't have approached it with more dignity and talent. The excitement just bubbled. People talk about that kind of magic. And if you think an audience is feeling that, how do you think I'm feeling?

—Tom Hughes

Donald O'Connor—one of Tom's favorite performers— in *Little Me*, 1964, with Rosie Holotik and Lynne Gannaway.

April 4, 1965
Dear Mr. Hughes,

I certainly do think plans for my summer are shaping up nicely. If you'll remember, on our plane trip to New York we were discussing how wonderful it would be to get one engagement away from Dallas. I think you'll agree with me in saying you show great success as an agent!

I would have brought the contracts by your office Saturday but I didn't get to my house until the afternoon. I will bring them by around 11:30 this coming Saturday, at which time I hope to have the additional pictures you need.

Although you could easily tell by my ooo's and ah's that I loved every minute of my trip, I just have to put in writing that it is one week I don't think I shall ever forget. I honestly can't imagine having a more beautiful, magical time. Besides, you brought me to the final realization of what I want to do with my life.

I certainly hope to see you Saturday. If not then, maybe another time before auditions will present itself. Talk about a strange feeling—to sit in the audience and watch people being cast as members of the chorus I'm going to miss this summer!

Please say hello to Mrs. Rodgers for me and tell her my hair is coming along fine.

I hope you enjoyed your trip to the Awards—as I'm sure you must have!

I assure you, Mr. Hughes, there is no displeasure here! If you told me I was to have a three-week engagement reading poetry at the Dallas Y.W.C.A., I would rest assured you had a good reason and that it was for the best!

Sincerely,
Sandy

By 1965, Sandy Duncan was well-known to Dallas audiences, but Tom believed she could have a national career. Tom and Margaret Rodgers, the Musicals co-producer, took 19-year-old Sandy to New York for auditions, hoping to help her find her first job outside North Texas. Those auditions led to four summer jobs around the country and Sandy's decision to make the theatre her life, as she explains in this thank-you note. She has credited this trip with launching her career.

Sandy Duncan, mid-1960s, around the time
of her 1965 career-launching trip to New York with Tom and coproducer Margaret Rodgers.

Tom and Ann Blyth, who starred in the *King and I* with Michael Ansara, 1965.

Tom and John Tedford in the 1970s.
John served as music director for Dallas
Summer Musicals 1962-73 and toured
with shows throughout the U.S. and
Canada.

Tom with Pat Suzuki, in town for *Flower Drum Song*, 1966. Pat starred in the Broadway show during its 1958-1960 run and in the remounted show Tom produced in Dallas.

Celeste Holm with Tom at the opening night party for the 1967 State Fair Musicals' presentation of *Mame*.

Douglas Fairbanks, Jr. played the role of Henry Higgins in the Musicals' 1968 production of *My Fair Lady*. He autographed his picture: *"To my good friend Tom Hughes whose advice, wisdom, and faith made my success in Dallas possible. — Doug"*

Constance Towers Gavin and Michael Allinson in *The Sound of Music*, 1968. Connie and Tom remained close friends throughout his life. She was especially delighted when the children arrived and she became "Aunt Connie."

Tom's formal publicity portrait, 1968.

Tom with Dorothy Malone, starring in *Little Me* with Harvey Korman, 1970.

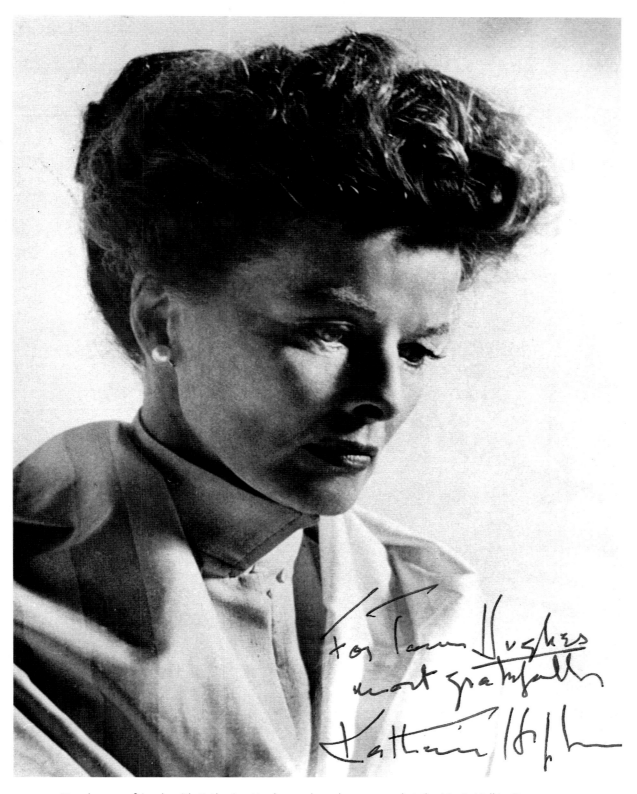

Tom became friends with Katharine Hepburn when she appeared at the Music Hall in *Coco*, 1971.
She gave him her headshot and autographed it: *"For Tom Hughes, most gratefully Katharine Hepburn."*

In 1972, Dallas Summer Musicals came to a halt for a major renovation of the Music Hall. Tom had realized for years that renovations would be necessary for Dallas to continue to attract top talent and he had discussed the theatre with many of the stars he brought to town. In particular, he corresponded extensively with Mary Martin about the Music Hall. After she publicly mentioned the need for an improved theatre in a 1967 interview, Mary wrote to Tom:

I was probably overly optimistic that someone should speak up and attempt to stimulate definite action towards the building of a theatre that would truly represent one of the largest and richest cities in the country. . . Of course, I am sorry if my expression has not been of any constructive help. Perhaps I should crawl back in my old-fashioned corner and try to be silent like a young lady was taught to be. But I can't! . . . Perhaps it would be more constructive if I approached the problem from another standpoint. Has an organization been formed? Have contributions been solicited? Or is this the time to start? . . . This is an important problem, one that I sincerely would like to help solve.

Tom believed the best solution for Dallas at that time was to renovate the Music Hall, not to build a new theatre elsewhere in the city. Many others disagreed, but Tom wasn't afraid to speak up. In 1967, the City of Dallas approved the bond package for the Music Hall's 1972 renovations.

Years after the work was completed, Leon Rabin—avid Dallas arts enthusiast and supporter—told *The Dallas Morning News*:

There would be no Music Hall in Fair Park except for Tom Hughes. Many people in the Dallas community had rejected Fair Park as a place for cultural activity. They thought a new hall should be somewhere else . . . It was Tom who articulated the important reality that no matter where the Music Hall might be in the future, right now, the only place was Fair Park. His presentation to the city council and community rallied support.

Tom oversaw the entire project, every detail from beginning to end. He went to work in a hard hat every single day that year—on top of his three-piece suit and his cane, of course! I'm sure there were numerous headaches, near misses, and all the frustrations of any construction project. But he never let those problems distract him from his excitement about the end goal.

He described the Music Hall during renovation in a letter to his friend Jack Lee, famed Broadway conductor and music director. Jack worked with Tom as music director for Dallas Summer Musicals in 1964 and several subsequent seasons. Tom wrote:

You would not recognize it at the moment for there is nothing left but a bare shell of four exterior walls and a roof. The renovation program is truly exciting and on completion we will not really have a renovated or remodeled theatre, but actually a new theatre.

Three new wings are being added, double dressing and rehearsal space, a main entrance that will be elaborate and exciting. And a 250-seat restaurant area. Along with the needed essentials of new restrooms, air conditioning, new seats, modern stage equipment, we should have one of the finest facilities in the country come October.

The renovation also provided space for an indoor ticket office, a beautiful forty-foot-tall sculpted

In 1972, Tom managed the renovation project of the Music Hall, coming to work every day in his three-piece suit, with tie and cashmere scarf—and a hard hat. He hated to lose that summer season, but loved the end result: a venue Tom described as feeling neither remodeled nor renovated, but essentially brand new.

Tom showing John Davidson the Music Hall's renovation project, 1972.
John had starred in *Camelot* the previous year and returned the following year to play Curly in *Oklahoma!*

Tom touring Sandy Duncan through the Music Hall renovation, 1972. She is sitting on boxes containing the new auditorium seats.

You sit down in that seat for a production, and that house curtain goes up. Hopefully, we will wrap around you the wonderment of music, book, dance, voice. And at the end of two and a half or three hours, you walk out of the theatre, your step is lighter, your smile is broader, and you have had a remarkably wonderful evening. And if we can do that on every performance, then we have done our job.

—Tom Hughes
shown in the Music Hall after renovation, 1972

chandelier, and a new grand double stairway leading down to a reflecting pool.

The resized orchestra pit was fitted with a hydraulic lift system, and in the auditorium itself, the acoustics were substantially improved.

The only aspect of the renovation Tom had disliked—and disliked greatly—was the loss of the 1972 season.

So he was thrilled when the Music Hall reopened in October 1972 for the eighty-seventh annual State Fair of Texas—excited to get back to doing what he loved best, and ecstatic to hear the patrons respond so well to the "feels like new" venue.

During the next few years, Tom was thrilled to bring even more stars to the newly renovated theatre, including Herschel Bernardi, Angela Lansbury, Paul Lynde, and Debbie Reynolds.

He was especially proud to produce *Take Me Along* starring Gene Kelly in 1974, which he always considered one of his greatest accomplishments.

Tom, always a Gene Kelly fan, had set himself the goal of luring Gene back to the stage after a thirty-three year hiatus—and he did it.

The show opened to a standing ovation at the Music Hall and went on to a national six-city tour. Tom saved this May 3, 1974, letter from Gene, discussing the issue of shoes and costuming:

I met with Arthur Boccia [costume designer] on Wednesday and we settled about the shoes. He promised me some sketches this week. I explained to him that the two boys who danced with me should have complementary colors in their outfits, but not exactly the same—so it shouldn't look like a vaudeville act. At the same time we must be enough alike

Production carpenter Stuart Hale, Cecile Hale Geaslin (Stuart's sister), actor William LeMessena, production manager Harold Goldfaden and Tom at a dinner meeting, 1975. Bill, one of Tom's favorite actors, performed at the Music Hall numerous times in the 1960s and 1970s.

to fit well together. I'm awaiting the cassettes from Jack Lee [music director] and as soon as I hear them I'll let you know what I think.

A few weeks later, Tom wrote the following reply:

As I sit at my desk this Saturday morning leafing through a large assortment of VIP letters requesting special consideration for seats for Gene Kelly in TAKE ME ALONG it occurs to me that I should give you a status report on the weeks' events and also to once again thank you for creating so much theatrical excitement for our theatre.

Angela Lansbury starred in *Mame*, 1976. She appeared previously at the Music Hall in *Gypsy*, 1974.

Tom produced *Take Me Along* starring Gene Kelly in 1974, which he always considered one of his greatest accomplishments. Tom was proud to have lured Gene back to the stage after a thirty-three year hiatus, a return that made national headlines.

Take Me Along, a musical adaptation of Eugene O'Neill's *Ah, Wilderness!,*
opened to a standing ovation at the Music Hall and went on to a national six-city tour.

Herschel Bernardi starred as Tevye in *Fiddler on the Roof* for the Dallas Summer Musicals in 1973, 1978, and 1983.
The 1983 production launched a national tour. In addition to working together, Tom and Herschel were close personal friends.

Debbie Reynolds in *The Debbie Reynolds Show*, 1975. She starred in several other
Dallas Summer Musicals productions, including *The Unsinkable Molly Brown* in 1989.

Carol Burnett and Rock Hudson in *I Do! I Do!*, 1974, her third show at the Music Hall.

In 1975, Tom brought to Dallas the Broadway tour of *Hello, Dolly!* starring Pearl Bailey, and the two became instant friends. When our children were born, she always referred to herself as "Auntie Pearl."

Pearl Bailey starring as Dolly Gallagher Levi in *Hello, Dolly!*, 1975.

"He dresses so beautifully. Others come in jeans and sweatshirts. But my dear Tom is always so impeccable. That's the way his theatre is and his crew is. He's very respected by all of us."

—*Mitzi Gaynor*

Mitzi Gaynor, a crowd pleaser with an enormous fan base, was one of Tom's favorite performers. She headlined her own show at Dallas Summer Musicals seven times during Tom's tenure—1973, 1975, 1977, 1978, 1980, 1982, and 1984—more frequently than any other star. Three of her shows are among the Musicals' top ten attendance records: *The Mitzi Gaynor Show* in 1975, 1977, and 1978. She returned to the Music Hall in 2010 for the 70th Anniversary Curtain Call Gala Performance.

Tom loved not only the Music Hall and Dallas Summer Musicals, he loved theatre and the arts in general. He also loved Dallas, and he loved his university—doing everything he could for each one of those communities and institutions.

Although audiences could well have assumed Tom's job with the Musicals took every minute of his time and attention, for thirty-two years Tom volunteered to produce and direct an annual musical for the Kiwanis Club of White Rock Lake. In 1966, he even starred as Henry Higgins in the Kiwanis production of *My Fair Lady*. Henry Higgins was a role he identified with, and one he had always wanted to play.

Tom regularly worked with local public high-school theatre directors to help cast student productions. He attended auditions at Dallas' Bryan Adams, Kimball, Lake Highlands, and Woodrow Wilson High Schools, among others. He produced the National Football Foundation Gridiron shows and worked with Children's Medical Center, Girl Scouts, the Junior League, and local high-school theatre and speech tournaments.

In 1973, in a desire to support the drama department of North Texas State University, he asked Dallas actress Martha Gaylord—known at the time as the first lady of the Dallas stage—if she would come speak to the students. She told him she didn't do speeches, but she'd love to do a play to help raise funds.

So, Tom and Martha, along with a few others, presented a reading of *The Marriage-Go-Round*. It was a great financial success, resulting in Tom and Martha establishing the Gaylord-Hughes Scholarship, an annual award for undergraduate theatre students, funded with proceeds from an annual Gaylord-Hughes production. Numerous local theatre personnel supported the productions, including Ed DeLatte, founder and managing director of Dallas Repertory Theatre, and actress Rose-Mary Rumbley.

In 1984, Tom and Martha each received an honorary Doctor of Performance Arts degree from North Texas State University. The degrees are awarded to those whose extraordinary achievements add substantial knowledge to, or better, society as a whole. The university had awarded only two previous such degrees. It was an honor Tom greatly appreciated.

Tom received an honorary Doctor of Performance Arts degree from University of North Texas, 1984. The degrees are awarded to those whose extraordinary achievements add substantial knowledge to, or better, society as a whole.

From 1961 to 1993, Tom (shown backstage) volunteered his time to direct and produce musicals for the White Rock Kiwanis Club.

Tom as Henry Higgins, with Lennie Barnett as Mrs. Higgins and Ann Lamb as Eliza Doolittle
in the production of *My Fair Lady* for White Rock Kiwanis, 1966.

Tom at a 1975 luncheon for the Gaylord-Hughes Scholarship with Martha Gaylord; director of Gaylord-Hughes productions Ed DeLatte, and actress Rose-Mary Rumbley.

Tom with Martha Gaylord in the Gaylord-Hughes production of *In Praise of Love*, 1976.

Tom with Martha Gaylord in the Gaylord-Hughes production of *Cactus Flower*, 1980.

Tom, stage manager Harold Goldfaden, and Ginger Rogers, holding her tap shoes for *The Ginger Rogers Show*, 1977.

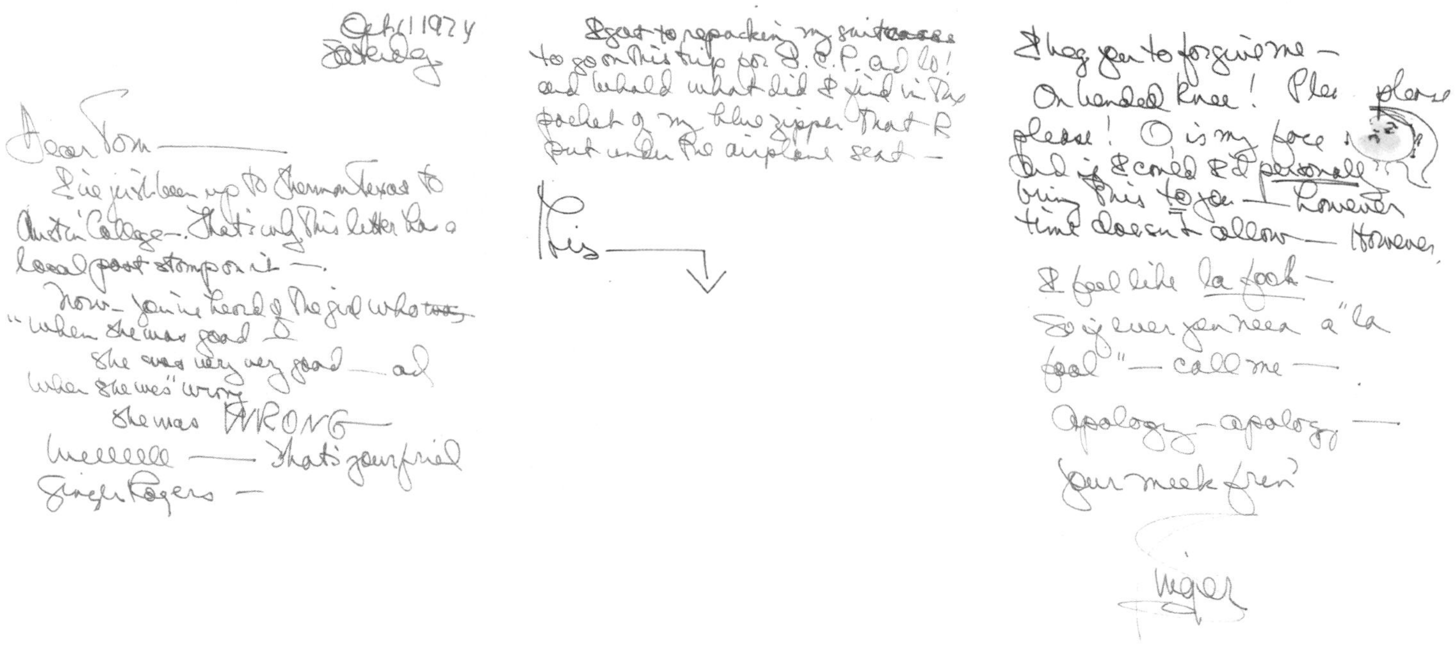

October 11, 1974
Saturday
Dear Tom—
I've just been up to Sherman Texas to Austin College. That's why this letter has a local post stamp on it—
Now you've heard of the girl who "When she was good, she was very very good, and when she was WRONG, wellllll—that's your friend Ginger Rogers.

I got to repacking my suitcases to go on this trip for J.C.P. [she was a spokesperson for J.C. Penney Co.] and lo! and behold what did I find in the pocket of my blue zipper that R put under the airplane seat—
This ⟶

I beg you to forgive me on bended knee! Please please please! O is my face [red] and if I could I'd personally bring this to you—however, time doesn't allow. However, I feel like la fool—So if ever you need a "la fool" call me—
Apology, apology—
Your meek fren'
Ginger

I don't know what Ginger Rogers lost when she was in town playing *No, No, Nanette*—and then found and sent back to Tom with this note. But I do know Tom was always the gentleman in his reply: "Dear Ginger, Many thanks for your wonderful letter of October 11th complete with poetry and cartoons. Your sweet and thoughtful comments will be treasured and you know that in my eyes you can do no wrong. Much, much love and all the best. Sincerely, Tom."

Paul Lynde and Beverly Sanders star in *The Best of Neil Simon*, 1980. Paul was a frequent presence at the Music Hall in the 1970s, starring in *Mother is Engaged*, 1974, and *The Impossible Years*, 1978, among others.

Tom continued to turn to his mentors for advice and counsel, as well as mentor those who came after him. He loved to pay it forward, to help guide others into the passionate work of theatre, whether on stage or behind the scenes. Actors, singers, dancers, musicians, stage managers, lighting directors—Tom took an interest in each person's career.

Not only did Tom help launch the careers of Sandy Duncan and Tommy Tune, he brought them both back to Dallas Summer Musicals numerous times over the years as their careers expanded to Broadway and beyond.

Sandy became an award-winning singer, dancer, and actor in theatre, television, and film. Tommy grew into an internationally acclaimed dancer, singer, actor, choreographer, director, and producer. Among his many accolades are ten Tony Awards, including the 2015 Award for Lifetime Achievement in the Theatre, and the National Medal of Arts, the highest award given to an artist by the United States.

Many others in the theatre also got their start on the Music Hall stage. Dallas native Kevin Ligon was cast in the Dallas Summer Musicals 1981 productions of *My Fair Lady* and *George M!* Jennifer Smith was in the chorus that same season, and the two became lifelong best friends. They both returned the following year in *The Unsinkable Molly Brown* and *Hello, Dolly!* with Carol Channing. Since their beginnings in Dallas, both Kevin and Jennifer have gone on to thriving Broadway careers.

Harold Goldfaden joined the Musicals in 1964 as a singer and dancer. Later, he became production stage manager and choreographer, and frequently traveled with Tom to New York and Los Angeles to assist with auditions. In the early 1990s, he became a production stage manager on Broadway. Tom often spoke of his great fondness and respect for Harold.

H. R. Poindexter was a theatre electrician whom Tom soon promoted to lighting director. H.R. met his wife, Sue Ann Erdmann, at the Musicals—she was a chorus singer and dancer. They gave Tom the honor of becoming godfather to their son, Larry. At Tom's encouragement, H.R. and the family moved to New York to work on Broadway, where H.R. won a Tony Award for lighting design in 1971. He then moved to Los Angeles to start a theatre with famed actor and producer John Houseman.

When H.R. died at 41, his son reached out to Tom, asking if he could audition for the Musicals chorus in 1978. Tom suggested he come to Dallas, but only with the understanding that Larry would have to win a role just like every other singer and dancer.

Not only did Larry win a role in rigorous competition that summer, but he came back to Dallas Summer Musicals for several years and went on to a highly successful career as an actor in television and film, and as a producer. In 2018, Larry became executive producer of the bound-for-Broadway musical, *The Cher Show*.

Tom also had some extraordinary staff members who stayed with him for years.

Peter Wolf designed sets and costumes for more than one hundred productions during thirty-five seasons in Dallas. During those years, he also designed sets for two national tours and fourteen Broadway shows. His Broadway credits include the 1979 revival of *Peter Pan* starring Sandy Duncan and Christopher Hewitt, which originated at Dallas Summer Musicals.

Gary Surratt joined as house manager in 1961 and became assistant managing director in 1963. By the mid-1970s, he was executive production associate and assisted Tom in running the day-to-day operations of the Music Hall, as well as managing finances. Not only did Tom and Gary work closely together for those years, they were also dear personal friends. Gary was Tom's best man in our 1983 wedding.

Stuart Hale, the production carpenter who virtually ran the backstage, stayed with Tom and the Musicals for decades. Patsy Neumann, wardrobe supervisor for thirty-five years, took over the position from her mother, Vivian Faucher, who had also worked with Tom and had served as wardrobe supervisor for fifty years.

Tom had a special gift for recognizing talent everywhere he looked. In 1973, Jean Marie Browne was the Musicals rehearsal pianist, and John Tedford was music director. The associate music director had recently been let go. Tom called Jean and told her that John was called away for a family emergency, and he needed her to conduct the orchestra for the upcoming Saturday matinee—a sold-out performance of *Fiddler on the Roof* starring Herschel Bernardi.

"I really wish I could help you, Mr. Hughes. But I've never conducted anything in my life," Jean told Tom. "I don't even own a baton."

"You know the show, Jean, and I know you can do this," Tom said. "Herschel has agreed to let you conduct the show."

Jean bought herself a baton, but there was no time to rehearse with the orchestra. Jean told her parents what she was about to do that weekend and begged them not to attend. They told her they wouldn't come, but they did. They were in the audience to see their daughter conduct a thrilling performance of *Fiddler* that Saturday afternoon—as was John Tedford.

When Jean exited the pit, she was shocked to see John there. "Congratulations, Jean. You were great."

"What are you doing here?" she asked. "How's your family?"

"Oh, everyone's fine. This was a test. Mr. Hughes wants to see you in his office."

Now, Jean was nervous. She thought the performance had gone fairly well, all things considered. Why did Mr. Hughes want to see her?

"You just passed quite a test, conducting the show like that, Jean," Tom said. "There was no emergency for John. It was a wonderful performance." Of course, Tom hadn't doubted the outcome of such a test; he never would have put the show at risk.

"Next year, Broadway conductor Jack Lee is returning to Dallas," Tom said. "And I need an associate music director and conductor to work with him. I'd like you for that position."

"I really appreciate that, Mr. Hughes. But I'd rather continue on as the rehearsal pianist," Jean told him.

Tom paused. Then he said, "Jean, that's not the job we're offering you."

Jean Browne served as Dallas Summer Musicals associate music director and conductor from 1974 to 1979. She assisted Jack Lee in fifteen productions, including the role of associate conductor in 1979 when Tom remounted *Peter Pan.*

Peter Pan went on to Broadway and a forty-two week national tour—with Jean Browne becoming the first woman to conduct a hit musical on Broadway.

The show received a Tony Award nomination for best revival. In addition, Sandy Duncan received a Tony nomination for best performance by a leading actress in a musical. The role also earned her a Drama Desk Award nomination for outstanding actress in a musical.

Famed Broadway director and Tom's close friend Lucia Victor, music director Jack Lee, choreographer Eivie McGehee, and associate music director Jean Marie Browne in rehearsal for *Gone With the Wind*, 1976. Tom recognized Jean's talent and encouraged her to take on more and more responsibility. In 1979, she became the first female to conduct a hit musical on Broadway.

Sandy Duncan in the 1979 Dallas Summer Musicals
production of *Peter Pan*. The show went on to Broadway,
earning two Tony Award nominations, and a national tour.
Sets by Peter Wolf.

Sandy Duncan seated center, meeting the crowds after a 1979 performance of *Peter Pan*. Sandy said Tom always accompanied the stars to the stage door when they met audience members and signed autographs. "He was there both as a presence and a protector."

Broadway actor and singer Laurence Guittard starred as Ashley Wilkes in the Dallas Summer Musicals production of *Gone with the Wind*, 1976, shown here with Leigh Beery as Melanie Wilkes. Tom produced the show in collaboration with famed Broadway director Lucia Victor and Pulitzer Prize-winning writer Horton Foote. Laurence also played in *Oklahoma!*, 1979, and *The Unsinkable Molly Brown*, 1982.

John Davidson had played Lancelot in *Camelot* many times, but Tom thought he was capable of playing Arthur. At Tom's urging, John successfully took on that role at the Dallas Summer Musicals, 1971.

In addition to *Peter Pan*, Tom brought many highly successful shows to the renovated Music Hall throughout the 1970s, including *Gigi*, *Mame*, *The Odd Couple*, *The Fantasticks*, *Cabaret*, and *Same Time Next Year* with celebrities including George Burns, George Chakiris, Carol Channing, Mitzi Gaynor, Rock Hudson, Jack Klugman, Vincent Price, Tony Randall, and Debbie Reynolds.

But even with a string of successes—and having played a significant role in the history of American musical theatre—a losing season comes along every now and then. For Dallas Summer Musicals, that season was 1976.

In fact, it was a losing year for summer musical theatre across the country. Tom knew his stars and shows were top notch—Angela Lansbury, George Burns, Carol Channing, *Mame*, *Funny Girl*, *Same Time Next Year*, *Oliver!*—but he thought maybe people were just too busy with the U. S. Bicentennial celebrations to think about theatre. Whatever the reason, Tom took it in stride, always the calm leader, examining what he could have done better, and looking ahead to the next season.

There was one bright star for Tom that season, however, and that was his production of *Gone with the Wind*. He was excited about the talent involved in adapting the story, based on the novel by Margaret Mitchell, to musical theatre. He collaborated with famed Broadway director Lucia Victor, composer and lyricist Harold Rome, music director Jack Lee, and Pulitzer Prize-winning writer Horton Foote, in addition to the Musicals' own local talent. He was always exceedingly proud of that show.

The following year, Dallas Summer Musicals made a lasting contribution to musical theatre when Tom worked with music director Jack Lee and *The Fantasticks'* original composer Harvey Schmidt to develop the show's first full orchestral score. The original music was created for piano and harp, with the harpist occasionally also playing percussion. In May 1977, Tom wrote to Jack Lee:

Dear Jackson:

It was a pleasure indeed to have the opportunity to be with you, if ever so briefly, while in San Francisco. Hopefully Gower [Champion] has stopped rehearsing by this time and the show has settled in for at least a while. I know it has been hectic for you, but also please know that you should be very proud of what has been accomplished. It is indeed "a 1970's ANNIE" and I am certain that three people made it happen, Debbie [Reynolds], Gower and you.

As promised, enclosed please find script and score of FANTASTICKS along with a cassette of a segment of the score as recorded by Arthur Fiedler with the Boston Pops. Certainly, it is only a small segment but will give you an idea of the rich wonderful sound which is possible.

We need to know as soon as possible the number of musicians you think would be best for FANTASTICKS, not necessarily the breakdown but the number in order that we can distribute personnel through the rest of the season.

The full orchestral score of *The Fantasticks* debuted at the Dallas Summer Musicals in 1977.

George Chakiris in *The Fantasticks*, 1977. The show—which has been called the world's longest-running musical, with more than 20,000 off-Broadway performances—was originally scored for just three instruments. Tom worked with the show's composer, Harvey Schmidt, and music director Jack Lee, to develop the show's first full orchestral score. The full score of *The Fantasticks* made its world debut in August, 1977, at the Music Hall.

The two stars of *In Person—George Burns & Carol Channing* at the Music Hall as part of their national tour, 1976.

Internationally known stage and screen legend Lauren Bacall starred in *Wonderful Town,* 1977.
In a note to Tom, she described the show's run at the Music Hall as "the best two weeks of the tour."

Dear Tom—

This is late in coming—I have been wanting to
write you since the day we left Dallas. It was the
best two weeks of the tour—and as long as you
are there—it will ever be thus I am sure.

Your ease in making it all work—everything
functioning at its best from backstage—stage—
days off—in all areas. It meant a great deal to
me—to all of us.

Your letter of farewell was the only one of its kind
I have ever received. And then to find your flowers
the first I gazed upon in St. Louis was too much. I
thank you for it all—I won't forget it.

And of course in the glory of those two weeks I
neglected to buy Summershine T-shirts. Could the
lady who handles them please send me two large
and I will send her a check? And you won't forget

the couple of pictures I had asked for—one in the
evening gown sitting on the stage on my way to
passing out in the last vignette—and of me upside
down in Conga—and one of me with George
only a smile instead of mouth gaping open. I hate
to ask you for anything after you had done so
much—but I want my own record in pictures of
"Wonderful Town." They were the only good ones
taken.

Please thank Peter for his sweet and funny
thought of me in St. Louis and give young David
a hug for me. Blenheim and I miss him. And fond
hellos to the Luptons.

I hope we do another one one day. I look forward
to it. Meanwhile—take care and let me know
when you'll be in New York.

Thank you—thank you—thank you—again and
again and again. Betty

Letter Tom received from Lauren Bacall after she starred in *Wonderful Town*, 1977, bringing her dog Blenheim with her to Dallas. In her
note—which she signed as Betty, her given name—she refers to receiving a letter and flowers from Tom. He always wrote thank-you
notes to the stars who performed in the Dallas Summer Musicals.

Lauren Bacall and
Molly Maloney in
Wonderful Town,
1977.

Katharine Hepburn's signed publicity photo from *A Matter of Gravity* 1977: "Tom, affectionately, Kate."

Tom presented Katharine Hepburn starring in *A Matter of Gravity* at McFarlin Auditorium
on the campus of Southern Methodist University in Dallas, 1977.

Dear Mr. Hughes

How very nice of you to give us such a nice welcome—Roses, whiskey and campari and your own kind attention at the theatre.

Thank you very much,
Katharine Hepburn

Dear Tom Hughes

Again my thanks for that huge bunch of red roses—I must say they [the audience] seemed to have a good time which is always a great relief—and were generous with their laughter and attention. Now if it only were not so damp that my hair won't stay in curl—I should be happy as a lark.

Thank you,
K. Hepburn

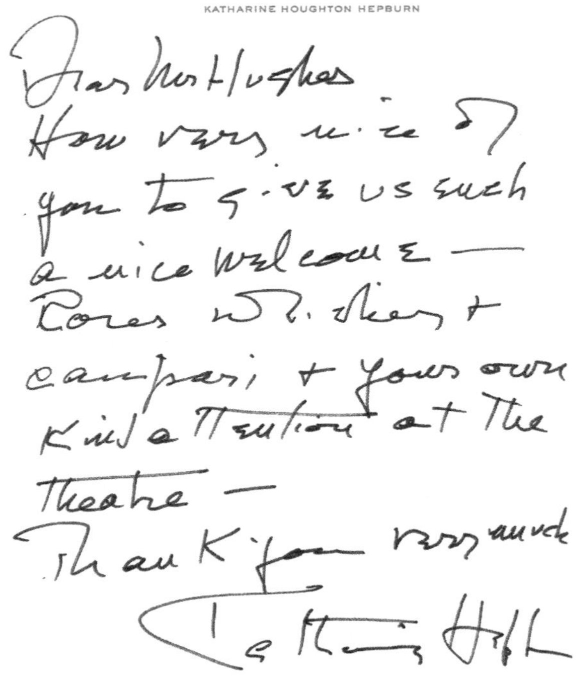

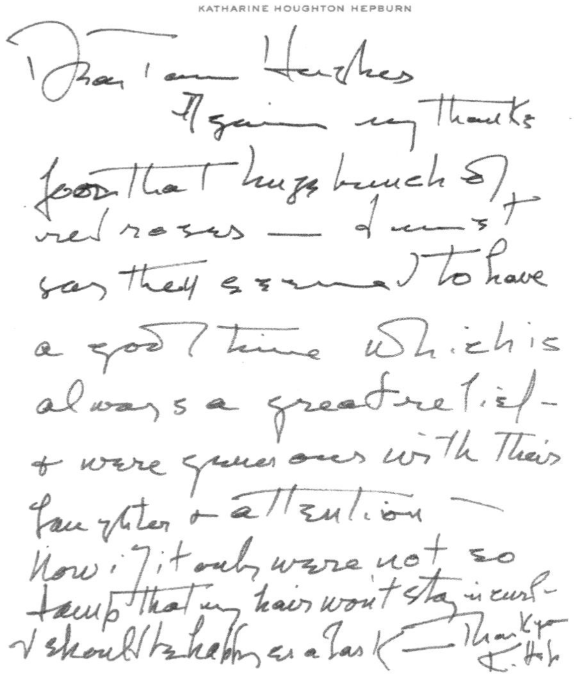

These notes from Katharine Hepburn to Tom reflect their growing friendship.
The first two notes were written when she came to Dallas to star in *Coco* in 1971.

II-15-1977
Dear Tom—

You are very sweet to have given me such a warm welcome. Flowers galore— whiskey galore—very pleasant to be on the receiving end. And the rooms are so pleasant.

Too bad we're not at the Music Hall. It is very worrying when they can't hear. Especially this play which has so many words.

Affectionately. Thanks.
Kate

II-23-1977
Tom—

That basket ! Those birds ! Those roast beef tid-bits. That paté. Those cold vegetables. That wine. That brie. That cut fruit. Those dishes— the silver—The napkins which we are wearing not using. The pastry. The cakes. The olives. The basket.

The LOOK OF TOTAL luxury—what can I say—What could anyone say—

Love. Love. Love.
Kate

We went well here. Got a good review for the play.

II - 15 - 1977

Dear Tom—
You are very sweet to have given me such a warm welcome. Flowers galore — Whiskey galore— Very pleasant to be on the receiving end. Think & enjoy. And the rooms are so pleasant.
Too bad were not at the Music Hall. It is very worrying when they can't hear. Especially this play which has so many words. Affectionate thanks
Kate

II - 23 - 1977

Tom -
That basket ! Those birds ! Those roast beef tid-bits. That pate. Those cold vegetables. That wine. That brie. That cut fruit. Those dishes - The silver - The napkins which we are wear--ing not using. The pastry. The cakes. The olives. The basket.
The LOOK OF TOTAL luxury - What can I say - What could anyone say -
Love. Love. Love.
Kate

We went well here. Got a good review for the play.

These two notes were written in 1977, when Katharine came to town to star in *A Matter of Gravity*, which Tom presented at McFarlin Auditorium on the campus of Southern Methodist University in Dallas.

I learned a great deal from Shirley MacLaine and Katharine Hepburn when they were here. They're both professional perfectionists. They give 100 percent and you know you can't do any more. That's what I want to try to do.

—Tom Hughes, 1977

The Shirley MacLaine Show was a "blockbuster three-day appearance" at the Music Hall in 1977, as described in *The Dallas Morning News*. *A Matter of Gravity* with Katharine Hepburn, also presented by Tom, opened on the campus of Southern Methodist University immediately after. As noted in the *News*, "this back-to-back star booking is truly a coup. Within the space of a week, Dallas has been given the rare opportunity of seeing a pair of America's premier theatre people." Shirley returned to the Music Hall again in 1983 and in 1990 (shown here).

Richard Burton   Friday Oct. 17th., 1980.

Dear Tom,

A brief note to thank you for your courtesy and care. The houses (theatre and habitation) are going to be greatly missed by us (that means) (& Susan too.). We genuinely hope to come back here one day and can well understand your deep attachment to Texas and above all to Dallas. We've caught a little of the Texan fever ourselves. Thank you again for every thing. Will you tell anyone who's interested that I've found the audiences here (almost without exception) to be the fastest, wittiest and most attentive of any I've faced — and that includes the Old Vic which hitherto had been my favorite? Thank you again - Susan joins me in sending warmest personal regards.

Sincerely

Richard B.

P.S. Don't we owe you some money?

Friday, October 17th, 1980
Dear Tom,

A brief note to thank you for your courtesy and care. The houses (theatre and habitation) are going to be greatly missed by us (that means Susan, too.). We genuinely hope to come back here one day and can well understand your deep attachment to Texas and above all to Dallas. We've caught a little of the Texas fever ourselves. Thank you again for everything. Will you tell anyone who's interested that I've found the audiences here (almost without exception) to be the fastest, wittiest and most attentive of any I've faced—and that includes The Old Vic which hitherto had been my favorite? Thank you again. Susan joins me in sending warmest personal regards.

Sincerely,
Richard B.
P.S. Don't we owe you some money?

Richard Burton in the role of King Arthur in the 1980 State Fair Musicals production of *Camelot*.

While Tom was weathering a tough season in 1976, the year was going great for me in Wichita Falls. I was a high-school senior that fall, preparing for my big college adventure. I had planned to attend Smith College in Northampton, Massachusetts, with designs to ultimately become an attorney like my father. I loved my hometown and my family, and I knew I would miss everyone terribly. I would especially miss Kenny, who was already a freshman at North Texas State University in Denton. But I also knew this was my opportunity to forge my own path. I was ready, and I was excited.

Kenny was home for winter break that year, and we had a fabulous time together—until Christmas Eve. That night, with the table set for Christmas Eve dinner, the entire family was gathered in the living room waiting for Dad. We waited and waited. It is never a good thing when an alcoholic is late arriving home, and every one of us was painfully aware of that.

Dad had totaled his car more than once, and we were always terrified he would kill someone in his next crash. So when the hospital called after seven o'clock to say he'd broken his hip in a car accident, we were almost relieved. That was it? No other injuries? No one else hurt? We assumed Dad's hip could be repaired and he'd be fine.

But during surgery the following week, my father suffered respiratory failure, and spent the following eight months in a coma.

Much of my time was spent sitting by his bed and talking to him during those months—never knowing if he could hear me. I made my peace with him, deciding to change my college plans and join Kenny at North Texas State. I couldn't possibly be so far away when my family was in such pain.

When my father died in August, I felt deeply grateful he was no longer suffering. I left for college the day after his funeral.

With Dad gone, my desire to be a lawyer seemed to just evaporate. My mother had been active in community theatre for years, and I'd always loved watching her perform. So I changed my major to drama, was cast in a play immediately, and realized that was the path for me.

Kenny turned 21 the last day of my freshman year. He and his friends were going to a Texas Rangers game for his birthday, and he invited me to come along. But my classes ended a few days earlier than his. I was worried about Mom at home alone, so I headed back to Wichita Falls as soon as I could, skipping the party.

The night of Kenny's birthday, the phone rang several hours after Mom and I had gone to bed, and I answered it in my room. A man introduced himself as an emergency-room doctor at John Peter Smith Hospital in Fort Worth. He wanted to speak to the parents of Kenny Kouri. I told him my mother was sleeping but that I could talk to him.

"I'm sorry to tell you that Kenny was involved in a one-car accident near Cleburn," he said. Cleburn is just south of Arlington, where the Rangers played. I realized Mom and I would need to drive out there right away, and my mind immediately started making plans.

"Kenny's injuries were quite serious," the doctor continued. "He was flown by helicopter to the hospital here. He suffered internal injuries that required surgery."

Oh. Worse than I'd first thought. I wondered how long we would need to stay in Fort Worth. How long would he be in the hospital?

My brother, Kenny, escorted me to the annual Wichita Falls Junior Forum Presentation, spring 1977.

"Kenny died on the operating table," the doctor said. "He expired. I'm so sorry."

He expired?

No. Credit cards expire. My vibrant, athletic, and hilarious brother did not expire. That wasn't possible.

But that was exactly what had happened.

I somehow managed to walk into my mother's room. She was sitting up in the bed, staring at me. As I told her the news, I watched her physically sink beneath the weight of her losses. I saw her leaving me, leaving us all behind, but I didn't know where she'd gone. In fact, my mother became bedridden in her grief, and it would be many years before she would recover.

Thankfully my Granny moved in to take care of my mother, and Aunt Leta and Uncle Ellis also helped. They had been our protectors for years, taking us in to live with them during summers, especially if my father's drinking had been particularly out of control. Aunt Leta cooked beautiful meals, played the piano, and sang the most gorgeous spirituals, always comforting us. Theirs was the bedrock marriage in my life.

I had such a deep love for Aunt Leta and Uncle Ellis. I trusted their judgment completely and felt safe leaving my mother in their strong hands. Without their help, I would not have been able to return to college.

Somehow the days of that summer passed one at a time as they always do, and in the fall, I returned to North Texas State for my sophomore year. It's not that college meant anything in particular to me at that point; I just didn't know what else to do.

I have very few memories from the next three years. I must have spent all my time studying because I received excellent grades. I think I mostly just floated along, trying to figure out who I was and how I could possibly live in this world without my brother.

By my senior year, I had started to feel a bit better, a bit more normal, my feet almost back on firm ground. Still, I don't remember much from that year, either. I know I played some tennis, acted in some plays and talked with friends. I know I signed up to coach a little girls' soccer team through the YMCA, but there was a mix-up and I was assigned to a little boys' football team. I have a few vague memories of football practices and games, and a few pictures.

Through that very long and very dark period, I have only one truly vivid memory: February 5, 1981, the night I met Tom Hughes.

I thought about Tom frequently in the days and weeks after I met him. He was funny and smart, and I had really enjoyed talking with him. As the follow-up to a humorous part of our conversation, I sent a large green plant to his dressing room, and he sent a nice and funny thank-you note in return. Still, I realized I'd probably never see him again.

Later that semester, I ran into a friend who had worked as Tom's assistant the previous summer. She wouldn't be available to work in the summer of 1981, and when Tom had asked if she knew anyone who could take her place, she'd suggested me.

"Oh, yes. I met her at a party," Tom had told her. "She had the most sparkling personality of anyone I've ever met." I confided to my friend that I felt exactly the same way about him.

"So, why don't you just call him up and go to lunch?" she suggested. Not knowing any better, I did just that. I found the phone number, called the Music Hall at Fair Park and asked for Mr. Hughes' office. I gave the secretary my name, and she put me on hold.

My sophomore year in college. Not long after my brother, Kenny, died, and two years before I met Tom.

David Cassidy, starring in *Little Johnny Jones*, 1981, was especially excited to perform at the Music Hall where his parents—Shirley Jones and Jack Cassidy—had performed years earlier.

Looking back, it's difficult to believe I ever did that! But I was just a young girl from Wichita Falls. I had never seen the Music Hall and had no knowledge of the role Tom Hughes played in the Dallas arts community. I had no idea that while I'd been in college, Tom had been working with Lauren Bacall, Shirley Jones, Liza Minelli, and dozens of other stars.

If I'd understood his position in the community, I'm not sure I would have summoned the courage to call him. I'd thought the Music Hall was probably just a slightly larger and possibly more upscale version of our own Backdoor Theatre in Wichita Falls. In fact, the night I'd met Tom, I'd shared with him that we had a playhouse in my hometown, too, and I tried not to sound too superior when I told him the house could seat almost 100! Tom had smiled and seemed genuinely happy for me.

When Tom came on the line, he said he was glad to hear from me. We talked briefly, and I asked if he would be available to go to lunch sometime the following week in Dallas. There was a long pause, and then he said he needed to check his calendar. I was on hold for quite a while.

Tom later told me he hadn't needed to check his calendar—he had needed to check his life. Tom's heart had been broken in college and he hadn't been romantically involved with anyone since. He was concerned that if he had lunch with me, his life might change forever, and that was not what he wanted. Tom loved his life exactly as it was, with the Musicals always coming first. He decided he couldn't risk the chaos of romance. He would tell me he was just too busy to get away.

When he came back on the phone, I could hear him take a deep breath.

"I'd love to go," he said.

The following week, we had a delightful three-hour lunch at the Cipango Club, one of Tom's favorite restaurants. After that lunch, we talked occasionally on the phone and sent each other amusing articles or items in the mail. Tom rarely called me, but always seemed happy to hear from me when I called him. He later explained he hadn't been comfortable initiating the calls because of our age difference.

When he found out I was about to be fired from my restaurant job as a pianist because I didn't know how to play "Happy Birthday," he sent me the sheet music to fifteen different versions of the song. I sent him a picture from my cat's birthday party. He helped me finish my final term paper on Malcolm X for my African-American History class. Tom and I were the greatest of friends—but nothing more.

Toward the end of that spring, Tom asked if I might be interested in becoming the front office assistant for the Musicals that summer. I certainly was! I joined the team right after graduating with a major in drama and minor in business. I worked alongside a good college friend, George Cooper, who was Tom's personal assistant and one of the most delightful guys I've ever known. We all had great fun that summer.

My responsibilities included helping around the office, running errands, and working on mailings and publicity for *Annie Get Your Gun, Juliet Prowse Show, Little Johnny Jones, George M!* and all the other exciting shows that season.

I also went with Tom to the airport when that season's stars—Rosemary Clooney, Florence Henderson, Martha Raye, and others—arrived for their shows. While we waited for their flights, we would sit in the Admirals Club and play gin rummy for money. We were avid competitors, and I know at one point I owed him more than $600. He later joked that I'd married him to get out from under my gambling debt! When the stars arrived, Tom would accompany them to their hotels in a limousine, and I would follow to make sure their luggage made it to the hotel.

On the Fourth of July, we were sitting in his office at the Music Hall playing gin after a performance. I was waiting to drive one of the actors back to the hotel. Tom seemed uncomfortable, which wasn't like him. I couldn't figure out what he had to be nervous about—I was the one already down several hundred dollars, and we hadn't even finished the third game yet.

Tom put his cards down. "Gin." Then he looked up at me. "And I love you and want to marry you."

He kissed me, and I kissed him back.

I was ecstatic and terrified—absolutely terrified. I felt our souls had recognized each other the moment we met. Yes, we both had so many reservations about our age difference. Nevertheless, we knew we were meant to be together, and our fears would just have to wait. We looked at each other and laughed.

It was all so absurd!

He was Tom Hughes, the eternal bachelor, internationally-known and respected producer of the Dallas Summer Musicals with decades of success in the business. I was Anné Kouri, a young girl from Wichita Falls with nothing but a black-and-white tabby cat and a recently acquired bachelor's degree. With such a disparity, our logical minds certainly might have thought better of our romance.

But from that moment on, we put our logical minds firmly in the back seat and let our hearts and souls take control. We were just along for the ride.

Although we kept our relationship strictly business at the office because we weren't ready to make it public yet, we had a wonderful few months. We went to dinners, movies, played more cards, and just enjoyed truly getting to know each other.

I was nervous about meeting Tom's mother, not knowing how she would react to her only son marrying after so many years. But as I stood on her porch for the first time with Tom by my side, she threw open the door and reached out to hug me.

"Get in this house!" she said to me. "I thought you'd never get here!"

Then, at the end of the summer, my mother and grandmother came to Dallas to meet Tom. They immediately recognized his kindness and sincerity, and they loved him. I was deeply happy. But when my grandmother returned to Wichita Falls and told Aunt Leta about my new love, my aunt was not impressed. Not being one to ever hold back her opinions, she got straight to the point in a phone call one evening.

"I understand from your grandmother that you're dating your boss."

That was not exactly the way I would have phrased it, but I answered, "Yes, ma'am. He's a wonderful man, and I love him. I believe he's the man for me."

Aunt Leta was silent. I desperately wanted her to understand how happy I was. But the longer she stayed silent, the more nervous I became. And with good reason.

"Anné Alexis Kouri, what kind of a foolish girl are you? Is this the way you were raised?"

"Aunt Leta. . ."

"Do you know how old he is?" she continued. "Have you lost your mind?"

In my New York City apartment, 1982. I moved to New York to pursue a career in theatre.

"But . . ."

"Your uncle and I did not raise you to throw your life away with a man more than twice your age!" She continued. "And do you know what truly disgusts me?"

I was silent.

"What really disgusts me is what your brother would think of you. It would sicken him."

Aunt Leta knew me well. She had cut me straight to the quick. When I could speak, I whispered, "What would you like me to do?"

"Get rid of him. And do it now."

I said the only thing I could say. "Yes ma'am."

The very next day I went into Tom's office and explained through my tears that I could no longer see him. He knelt beside me and listened. My heart was broken—and I had broken it myself. I was devastated.

Just a few weeks later, I heard that a friend was moving to New York to pursue an acting career. Without giving it another thought, I announced I was going, too.

I lived in New York for almost two years, auditioning for roles and working in a boot store called Texas on the Upper East side. It was not an easy time. But I dug deep within to battle the profound loneliness, daily rejection from auditions, and the lingering, oppressive grief of losing my father and Kenny. And I missed Tom, missed him badly. We were still friends who spoke daily, but the loss of the love I had hoped we would share filled me with pain.

I was cast in the role of Princess DeLong in the Dallas Summer Musicals production of *The Unsinkable Molly Brown*, 1982. Luckily for me, the costume needed to be remade that year, so I had the opportunity to wear a beautiful dress designed by famed costumer Arthur Boccia of Eaves-Brooks in New York.

The 1982 production of *The Unsinkable Molly Brown* starred Karen Morrow (seated, left). The cast also included Kevin Ligon, Linda Septien, Gary Henderson, Mary Jo Todaro, Shelley Hamrick Aubrey (second row), and me (far right).

In the spring of 1982, Tom traveled to New York on his annual trip to see plays and musicals for the following year's summer season. We had dinner together most nights, and I went with him to a few shows. I loved being with him.

One night he took a small ring box out of his coat pocket and handed it to me.

"Anné, will you marry me?" he asked.

I opened the box and saw the most beautiful emerald framed by two perfect diamonds. It was exquisite, but I knew I couldn't accept it. Tom was truly disappointed this time. We both cried. I told him I loved him, but that I could never marry him because of our age difference. I had finally accepted that we would have to remain just friends.

In December 1982, almost two years after Tom and I met, I decided to move back to Texas. At that time, I was considered a professional actor due to a brief appearance I had made in a soap opera called *Texas*. Consequently, I was asked to participate in the 1983 Gaylord-Hughes alumni show at North Texas State with Tom and Martha. I played the role of Pegeen Ryan in *Auntie Mame*.

It was good to see Tom, and he seemed finally at peace with our friendship. But during those rehearsals, I noticed he was spending his breaks speaking with an attractive cast member who was close to his age. And much to my surprise, I discovered I was not one bit happy about that. What in the world was she doing with "my" Tom?

While in Denton for the production, I stayed at the home of renowned former dean of women, Imogene Dickey Mohat. Imogene was a no-nonsense woman who had always been very close to Tom. I was sitting at her breakfast table on the day the play was scheduled to open, when Imogene simply reached over, handed me her telephone, and said with her usual authoritative tone, "Why don't you quit this nonsense? Call Tom Hughes and tell him you'll marry him."

I hadn't directly told her my true feelings for "Mr. Hughes," but she must have noticed I couldn't eat or sleep for thinking about him.

That's when it finally dawned on me that I could not wait one more minute to be with Tom Hughes. I called him and said I needed to see him. I went by his hotel suite that afternoon.

He asked why I dropped by, but I was so nervous I could hardly speak. I couldn't look at him. Staring straight down at the floor, I stuttered and started and stopped and barely got the words out.

"The reason I came here is that I have something I've wanted to tell you, but never could." I took a breath. "I just want you to know that I love you. I have always loved you from the moment we met."

This time, I took a deeper breath. "I wish I'd had the courage to follow my heart. I wish I had married you. I realize it's too late now. But I couldn't let you go one more moment without knowing how much I love you."

Tom did not say a word. I waited. Not one word. Finally, when I couldn't stand the silence any longer, I looked up.

He was seated with his arms folded and a thoughtful look on his face. He looked at me with those kind eyes, and a smile slowly spread across his face. He opened his arms to me.

"Welcome home."

We became engaged officially on February 14, 1983.

Tom and I at the opening night party for The Gaylord-Hughes production of
Auntie Mame, February 3, 1983. Although we had not announced it yet, we
had become engaged just a few hours earlier.

Tom at a 1982 planning meeting for the reopening of the Majestic Theatre as a performing arts venue, with ardent arts supporter Annette Strauss and Dallas mayor Jack Evans. Annette, who was elected Dallas mayor in 1987, served as both president and chairman of The Arts Community Alliance (TACA). Tom served as director of Theater Operating Company, which managed the Majestic for the City of Dallas, beginning with its reopening in 1983.

Tom and I with Liza Minnelli at the opening night party for *Liza in Concert,* the first performance at the renovated Majestic Theatre, March 1983. Tom and I had become engaged the previous month.

Yul Brynner starring in *The King and I*, 1982.
Tom and "Mr. B," as Tom always called him, were good friends.

DALLAS SUMMER MUSICALS

March 18, 1985

Dear Yul and Kathy:

It would appear that the fates are kind, that at long
last our reunion could possibly take place. We have
been planning it, counting on it and anticipating it
for much too long, but now it would appear that Anne'
and I will be in New York for an entire week beginning
Sunday, March 31 and nothing would give us greater
pleasure than to have the opportunity to spend some
time with you.

I know that your schedule is an hectic one, but we
would love to take you for a bite of supper after the
show, invite you to lunch or just share a wonderful
moment of conversation following a performance. In
other words, your wish is our command and our schedule
is totally flexible.

Naturally, I am anxious to see the show and eager for
you to meet Anne', but most of all and I am sure quite
selfishly I am hungry to have the joy of seeing you
both.

With much love and warmest regards.

Sincerely,

Tom Hughes, Producer

Music Hall
P.O. Box 26188 Dallas, Texas 75226 214/565-1116

March 18, 1985

Dear Yul and Kathy:

*It would appear that the fates are kind, that at long last our
reunion could possibly take place. We have been planning it,
counting on it and anticipating it for much too long, but now
it would appear that Anné and I will be in New York for
an entire week beginning Sunday, March 31 and nothing
would give us greater pleasure than to have the opportunity
to spend some time with you.*

*I know that your schedule is a hectic one, but we would love
to take you for a bite of supper after the show, invite you
to lunch or just share a wonderful moment of conversation
following a performance. In other words, your wish is our
command and our schedule is totally flexible.*

*Naturally, I am anxious to see the show and eager for you
to meet Anné, but most of all I am sure quite selfishly I am
hungry to have the joy of seeing you both.*

With much love and warmest regards.
Sincerely,

Once we had finally decided to spend the rest of our lives together, we needed to set a wedding date and plan a wedding. Tom had only one question about the wedding: Would it be before or after the summer season? I knew I would always share my husband with the Dallas Summer Musicals—that year and every year. I was so proud of Tom and his vast accomplishments that his devotion to his work never bothered me. That was the man I had met, and that was the man I loved.

Many of Tom's friends were thrilled by our engagement, and some were simply stunned. They had known him as a bachelor for such a long time. They weren't sure he would ever "take the plunge." Tom had received many monikers in the press and by those who knew him well—dapper impresario, the grand seigneur of musical theatre, the gentleman producer, the Ziegfeld of Fair Park, suave, urbane—but "romantic" had never been on the list.

Being formally engaged to Tom brought incredibly exciting and wonderful experiences into my life. We had intimate dinners with Yul Brynner, Liza Minelli, Mitzi Gaynor, and many other celebrities in some of the most beautiful restaurants in New York, Los Angeles, and London. I had the pleasure of meeting many of the fascinating people Tom brought to Dallas during the years we spent together: Eydie Gormé, Joel Grey, Richard Harris, Florence Henderson, Steve Lawrence, Liberace, Ann-Margret, Alexis Smith, Ben Vereen, and dozens more.

Years later, I looked back and wondered why I didn't appreciate those special experiences more at the time. Then it struck me: In my eyes, all those fine-dining experiences with famous actors paled in comparison to simply being with Tom. No matter where we were or whom we were with, the most interesting person in the room to me was always Tom Hughes. The sheer electricity that I felt in his presence seemed to outshine any other experience. At all times, he remained the kind, calm gentleman, no matter what was going on around him. He never needed to be the center of attention. Nevertheless, I felt such excitement in his presence—he was always the center of *my* attention.

It was during our engagement period that we visited with Tom's friends Mitch Leigh and his wife, Abby, in New York City. Mitch was a successful Broadway producer and the composer of *Man of La Mancha*. Tom had previously told Mitch I played the piano, and Mitch asked me about it during dinner one night.

"I've played for years, since I was 4 years old," I told him. Piano is one of my many loves. "In fact, I'm studying with a teacher in Dallas right now."

He nodded and asked simply, "Do you consider yourself a Baldwin person or a Steinway person?"

Those pianos were so far out of reach, I almost laughed. Tom and I were considering a Kawai, a good instrument in our price range. But I replied immediately, "I am a Steinway person."

Not long after that, back in Dallas, I answered a phone call from Whittle Music Co. saying I needed to come down to the store to pick out my Steinway, courtesy of Mr. and Mrs. Mitch Leigh. Pretty funny! I wondered which one of my friends was behind that joke. Tom, too, didn't quite believe it, until a mutual friend confirmed to him, "Some people give a crystal vase for a wedding gift. Mitch gives Steinways."

I was overwhelmed. I went down to Whittle's to test out several pianos and chose the beautiful ebony baby grand that continues to grace our home today. My children and I have spent thousands of enjoyable hours at that lovely piano. I will always be grateful to Mitch and Abby.

Tom and I at a dinner during our engagement.

Tom and I were married September 17, 1983, at Saint Michael and All Angels Episcopal Church in Dallas. It was the happiest day of my life. The love from our extended families was palpable. In fact, Tom, my mother, and Granny were old friends by that time because Tom had stayed in touch with them "behind my back" since the first time they met. Through our breakup, heartache, and friendship, Tom had continued to talk to my family, regularly calling Wichita Falls to see how I was doing. Of course, he won their hearts.

Most importantly, he won over Aunt Leta and Uncle Ellis. In fact, Aunt Leta later apologized to me.

Soon after our wedding, Tom invited Aunt Leta and Uncle Ellis to Dallas to celebrate their fiftieth wedding anniversary at the French Room in the Adolphus Hotel. Aunt Leta was a fine cook herself and was fascinated with the art of food. They were both delighted.

The next morning, as I walked her to the car she said, "Oh, Anné, I almost ruined your life! I'm so sorry I didn't understand. But thank God you and Tom found each other."

I was relieved to have her blessing, of course. But I also knew she'd been trying to protect me. She explained that when she'd heard the word "producer," she'd immediately assumed he was a Hollywood stereotype, complete with gold chains and a different woman every night. Of course, she'd want to protect me from that. And even with all the pain it caused me, I absolutely understood her motive was my best interest.

The day after our wedding, Tom and I left for our honeymoon in Bermuda. One afternoon while there, we were walking back into our hotel when I mentioned how unusual it was to be in public with Tom and not have anyone recognize him and come over to talk. But just as I said that, I heard "Tom Hughes!" We looked up to see a woman leaning over the lobby balcony.

"Aren't you Tom Hughes from Dallas?"

Tom said hello and waved. He was all smiles.

She waved back and called out, "My husband and I just love the Musicals!"

Two thousand miles from home, wearing sunglasses and a golf hat instead of his usual three-piece suit and the ubiquitous cane, Tom was still recognizable. He never minded visiting with a fan of the Musicals, talking about past shows or discussing the upcoming season, whether in the middle of a meal—or even on his honeymoon.

If someone were a fan of the Musicals, Tom figured he and that individual shared a love of theatre. And that's something he always appreciated.

The "honeymoon fan" in Bermuda might have been one of the few people to ever see Tom without his trademark cane. I'll bet she wondered where it was! He started carrying a cane when a woman on staff at the Musicals asked him what he would like from her upcoming vacation. For some reason, he asked for a cane. She said she would bring him one, with the stipulation that if she did buy him a cane, he had to walk with it. He agreed.

Tom's cane collection eventually grew to over 125—from canes that concealed swords or knives, to one with a wicker basket for gardening, and one with a hidden flask. He received canes from Liberace, Debbie Reynolds, Ginger Rogers, Tommy Tune, and so many others. Sandy Duncan gave him a sentimental cane that had belonged to her grandfather. Yul Brynner bequeathed a special gold-handled cane to Tom. Decade after decade, Tom was rarely, if ever, seen in public walking without a cane.

New acquaintances might ask if everything was all right. Even old friends would sometimes wonder aloud why he needed a cane. Had there been an accident at some time? An illness?

Tom never minded people asking, and he always gave them the same honest answer.

"I have a slight disease," he would say. "It's called af-fec-ta-tion."

After a slight hesitation, laughter would break out all around. Tom was a man who took his work extremely seriously—but never himself. He never minded a smile at his own expense.

Katharine Houghton Hepburn

Miss Katharine Hepburn
regrets that she is unable to accept
the kind invitation of
Mrs. Philip Salem Kouri
to the marriage of her daughter
Anné Alexis
to
Mr. Thomas Lloyd Hughes
Saturday the seventeenth of September.

VIII-22-1983

Tom and I were married September 17, 1983.

We were married at Saint Michael and All Angels Episcopal Church in Dallas.

My family was in attendance, and genuinely happy for us.

Tom and I on our honeymoon in Bermuda. Even wearing sunglasses and a golf hat, and without his three-piece suit and ubiquitous cane, we heard a woman from the hotel balcony yell, "Aren't you Tom Hughes from Dallas? My husband and I just love the Musicals!"

Tom, Martha Gaylord (center), and I in the Gaylord-Hughes production of *The Matchmaker*, 1985.
Tom and Martha starred as Horace Vandergelder and Dolly Gallagher Levi. I played the role of Mrs. Irene Molloy.

Having Tommy and Sandy back at the Music Hall is like having the kids home from college.

—Tom Hughes

Tommy Tune and Sandy Duncan starred in *My One and Only* at the Music Hall in 1985. Tom helped these two superstars get their start in theatre twenty-five years earlier, and remained good friends with both throughout his life.

My One and Only, 1985. Tommy Tune with Charles "Honi" Coles (above) and with Sandy Duncan (right).

Mary Martin and Carol Channing in *Legends*, part of the Majestic Broadway Series presented by Tom, 1986.

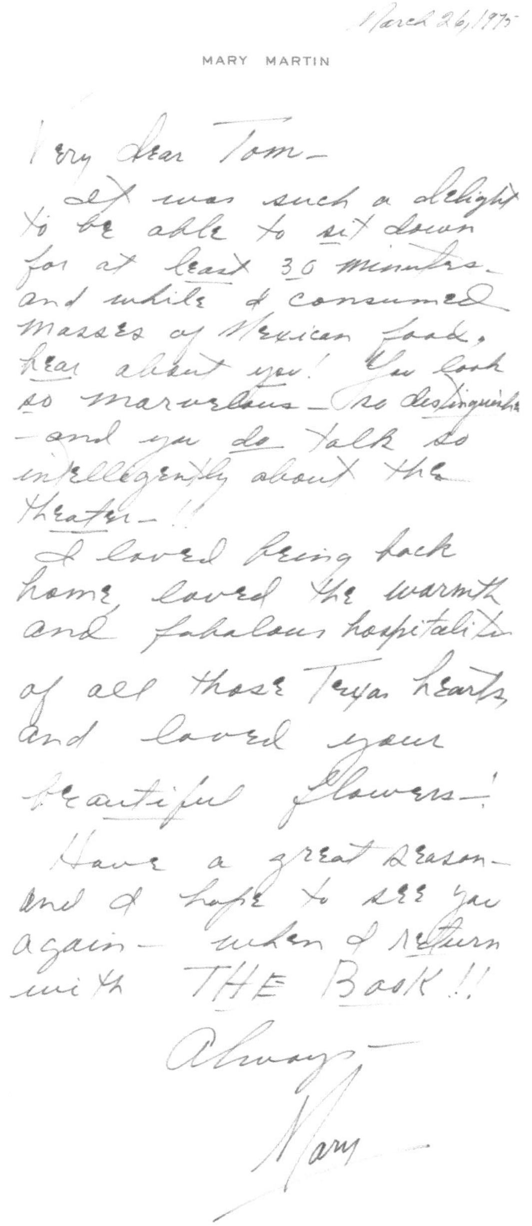

March 26, 1975

MARY MARTIN

Very dear Tom—

It was such a delight to be able to sit down for at least 30 minutes and while I consumed masses of Mexican food, hear about you! You look so marvelous—so distinguished—and you do talk so intelligently about the theater—!!

I loved being back home, loved the warmth and fabulous hospitality of all those Texas hearts, and loved your beautiful flowers—!

Have a great season—and I hope to see you again—when I return with THE BOOK!!!

Always—

Mary—

Mary Martin
March 26, 1975

Very dear Tom—
It was such a delight to be able to sit down for at least 30 minutes and while I consumed masses of Mexican food, hear about you! You look so marvelous—so distinguished—and you do talk so intelligently about the theater—!!

I loved being back home, loved the warmth and fabulous hospitality of all those Texas hearts, and loved your beautiful flowers—!

Have a great season—and I hope to see you again—when I return with THE BOOK!!!
Always—
Mary

Mary Martin and Tom met in 1947 when she opened her national tour of *Annie Get Your Gun* at the Fair Park Band Shell. She worked with him several times over the years, and they remained friends.

Tom and I modeling in a 1986 fashion show to benefit the National Kidney Foundation of North Texas, one of the many community organizations Tom supported.

Tom, Fritz Holt, and Keene Curtis. Keene starred in the 1985 production of *La Cage Aux Folles*, and Fritz, who served as stage manager, later produced a national tour of the show.

Tom and I with Phyllis Diller, in town for her one-woman show at The Majestic Theatre, 1984.

Dr. Honor Franklin and Dr. Bobby Mitchell with Gloria Vanderbilt (center) at a benefit event for the Dallas Summer Musicals Guild, 1985. Honor and Bobby were Guild members, board members, and longtime supporters of the Dallas Summer Musicals and Tom.

Liberace first came to the Music Hall to star in *The Great Waltz*, 1956. Shown here in town for *The Liberace Show*, 1984, with Tom and me.

Tom and I built a wonderful life together. For the first few years, we traveled quite a bit, enjoyed theatre, and spent time with wonderful friends. In addition, I started a career in commercial real estate. I thoroughly enjoyed the commercial real-estate world from the day I started, and Tom encouraged me every step of the way. At times when I wasn't sure about my own capabilities, Tom believed in me. I knew I was lucky to have married a man who saw the best in me and helped me become the best person I could be, day after day, year after year. That was Tom.

Just a few years after we married, Tom and I entered the glorious world of parenting. We were blessed with Kenneth Thomas in 1986, Ryan Alexis in 1988, and Kyle Elizabeth in 1992. Tom was a nurturing, devoted, and loving parent, and savored every moment of it.

Tom had waited such a long time to marry and start a family, he often told me he was amazed by his good fortune. He also told anyone else who would listen.

Although I traveled with Tom less often after the children were born, I still went with him to auditions in New York and Los Angeles whenever possible. I loved seeing the talent and being with Tom in his element. Even with so much riding on his decisions, he maintained the calm, composed, polite demeanor he was so well known for throughout the theatre world.

David Hansen, Dallas Summer Musicals production stage manager in the 1980s, remembers Tom always taking the time to see anyone who asked to visit with him during those out-of-town auditions, always greeting each person with enthusiasm and warmth. David's job was to keep everything on schedule. But people were always the most important aspect of theatre to Tom; the schedule could wait.

As far as I know, there was only one visitor who got Tom's attention completely off track at the auditions. Tony Randall and Tom had met in 1975 when Tom brought the national touring company of *The Odd Couple* to Dallas, starring Tony Randall and Jack Klugman. They had remained friends, and Tony stopped by the audition studios to visit in 1987. As part of the conversation, Tom mentioned that our son, Kenny, had recently started walking. That reminded Tony of a joke.

"So this man proudly told his friend, 'My son started walking at six months!' To which the friend replied, 'Oh, really? So where is he now?'"

The minute Tony finished the punch line, he and Tom both started laughing. And the more they laughed, the funnier they thought it was.

I was with Tom at those auditions, and I just didn't think the joke was all that funny. But the more they looked at me just sitting there and not laughing, the funnier it became to them. Eventually, the two of them were doubled over in hysterics. I never did think the joke was that funny, but it *was* a lot of fun to see two grown men—two very respectable grown men—completely out of control with laughter.

Wherever he went, Tom talked about his children and carried an embarrassing number of family photos, never hesitating to show every single one of them. No one was safe from his reports on his babies' latest gurgles or words, or the latest accomplishments of the children as they grew. When "Mr. Hughes" was at home with the family, he was all Daddy, all the time.

Completely involved in their lives, Tom would change, bathe, and dress the children, make them

Tom and Kenny at the Music Hall, June 1986. Kenny was 2 months old when we began our family tradition of taking the children to the Music Hall for dinner every Friday night each summer.

Tom with Kenny, 15 months.

Tom with Ryan, 1989.

breakfast, and when they became school-aged, check backpacks for homework and drive carpool. He wanted them to have the best education possible and be in a parochial setting, so their faith would be part of their daily studies, not just something they learned about at home and on Sundays. I felt the same way, and I know the children did benefit.

With his theatrical nature, he was a never-ending source of stories leading to hysterical laughter and the ever-present, "Again, Daddy! Do it again!" Their favorite seemed to be his rendition of *Peter Pan*, in which he played the parts of both Captain Hook and Mr. Smee. That one never got old!

Tom also gave each child special attention and time. Tom and Kenny created an absolute empire of Lego creations. And every week, the two of them had "boys' night out," usually a delicious ice cream at the local Swenson's.

With a friend's help, Tom built a gorgeous Victorian dollhouse for Ryan. While the house itself was an amazing creation, even more wonderful were the hours Ryan and Tom spent together on the floor playing with the dolls, the little furniture, and all the accoutrements.

As for his baby girl, he would hold Kyle in his arms and whirl her around the house singing "Some Enchanted Evening" in that beautifully rich voice of his. Judging by her smiles and gurgles, he won her over every time.

I loved seeing Tom crawl around on the floor with the children, all of them thoroughly enjoying each other. Watching him open up like that was even more special because I knew so well the buttoned-up image he maintained at work—especially in his office.

Tom's office, in the basement of the Music Hall, was dominated by an enormous and intricately carved chair given to him by the actor John Davidson and his wife in 1971. John had played Lancelot in *Camelot* quite a few times, but Tom thought he was ready to take on the role of King Arthur. It took Tom six months to convince John to try the part, and when he finally played it, he absolutely shone. After the show, he and his wife saw the chair in a gallery in Fort Worth. They sent it to Tom with a note that read: "Every Pope deserves his throne." It sat in Tom's office for years, flanked by two carved lions, a gift from Yul Brynner, from the set of *The King and I*.

The "throne," the lions, his collection of canes, the huge desk, and Tom's formal tone caused one writer to describe his office as "a cross between a nineteenth-century funeral parlor and a slightly down-in-the-heels club for English gentlemen." It all contributed to a very serious ambiance, which is exactly what Tom preferred at work. He might have shown everyone his babies' pictures when fifty or sixty people came by to socialize at intermission, but there was a line of formality he never crossed. There was no coming to work in jeans and a T-shirt for Mr. Hughes.

As Mitzi Gaynor said of him, "He dresses so beautifully. Others come in jeans and sweatshirts. But my dear Tom is always so impeccable. That's the way his theatre is, and his crew is."

Mitzi was one of the few people around the theatre who called him Tom. To almost everyone else, he was Mr. Hughes. Even I never called him Tom.

The gallant gentleman I met at that opening-night party in 1981 was Mr. Hughes. When we first started dating, I knew I couldn't continue to refer to him so formally, but neither could I quite get myself to call him Tom, although he'd asked me to. So, I called him by his initials, TLH, through our dating, breakup,

Tom bringing baby Kyle home from the hospital, 1992.

Clockwise from upper left: Kenny's baptism luncheon, 1986; Tom with Ryan and Kyle, 1992; celebrating Christmas 1988 with Kenny and Ryan; Ryan with her Daddy, 1989.

friendship, engagement, and wedding. Then, after watching the movie *All About Eve* together one evening, we started calling each other Bride and Groom. And through our entire marriage, those were the names we used.

Actors and celebrities who performed in Dallas loved "Mr. Hughes" for his formality, even keel, serious nature, and attention to detail. Mr. Hughes was in charge, and you could count on it. Those who came to Dallas to work with him appreciated that focused dependability and serious persona.

As Sandy Duncan said, "Tom gave himself and everyone around him a certain dignity. Everyone in and around his shows was always on their best behavior."

And that's the reason Stephen Lehew was so curious about some unusual noises at the Music Hall one summer night in 1989. Stephen was a well-known Broadway performer who was in town that year to perform the role of Jesus in *Godspell*. He tells a wonderful story about putting on his performance makeup and hearing unusual, sing-song sounds, almost like cooing. The sounds were coming from wardrobe and the voice sounded remarkably like Tom Hughes. Stephen couldn't imagine what was happening. Eventually, he put down his makeup brushes and walked to the wardrobe room.

It was Tom Hughes, with a beautiful baby on his lap.

"Who's my precious girl?" Tom was saying in that beautiful trademark baritone. He held baby Ryan up to his face. "Is that my sweet baby? Yes, she is. That's my precious girl."

When Tom looked up and saw Stephen in the doorway, he smiled and introduced him to Ryan. This was a side of Mr. Hughes that Stephen had never seen.

He has said it was a sweet moment he would always remember.

That might have been the first time one of the actors saw "Mr. Hughes" cooing with one of his babies, but it was certainly not the first time the children had been to the Music Hall.

From the time Kenny was an infant, we would have dinner with Tom every Friday night during the summer season at the Crystal Terrace Restaurant, and then go backstage together. While Tom would perform last-minute show checks, the kids and I would visit Patsy Neumann in wardrobe. "Aunt Patsy," as the children came to know her, was warm and welcoming. The kids felt this was their home away from home.

Aunt Patsy collected anything related to pigs, including a wonderful cookie jar that "oinked" when it was opened. Not surprisingly, that was the kids' single favorite item backstage, and Aunt Patsy always stocked it with little cookies and treats for them. They loved spinning in her chairs and looking at—but never touching—her sewing machines. Most of the cast and crew's backstage socializing centered around the wardrobe, and the children were thrilled to be a part of it all. As they grew older, they loved looking at Aunt Patsy's pictures of the stars and pointing to the people they knew. They would occasionally watch the cast put on makeup—although those painted faces did lead to some serious screaming when a stage-ready member of *Cats* surprised 8-month-old Kenny!

The kids also became close with production carpenter Stuart Hale. "Uncle Stuart" often gave the kids a backstage tour or let them play among the large travel cases stored behind the set. And there were other perks as well. One night before the house opened, Shirley MacLaine took Kenny and Ryan onto the stage with her and introduced them to her drummer, Cubby, from the original *Mickey Mouse Club*. The band broke into a spontaneous and rousing version of the "Mickey Mouse Club March," which absolutely thrilled the kids, who were very serious Mickey fans.

After Tom checked everything for the show, he would go out front to check on the box office. The kids and I would say goodnight to Aunt Patsy and Uncle Stuart and find seats in the last row of the theatre.

When the audience was seated, and the lights came down, we would watch Tom make his curtain speech and then listen to the overture. Afterwards, we would slip out and meet Tom in the lobby. He would load us into our car, hug and kiss everyone goodnight, and then remain at the Music Hall until closing.

I am eternally grateful for the wonderful memories of such a treasured summer ritual.

Tom was blessed to work with scores of wonderful actors and celebrities during his career. He developed long-term relationships with many, bringing some to perform at the Music Hall in several shows.

He had drawers filled with personal thank-you notes from performers who recognized Tom's passion for musical theatre and loved it as he did—performers including Katharine Hepburn, Richard Burton, Mary Martin, Pearl Bailey, and Ginger Rogers, among many others.

Mitzi Gaynor, a crowd pleaser with an enormous fan base, was one of Tom's favorites, and he brought her to Dallas Summer Musicals seven times during his tenure, more frequently than any other star.

But I think it's safe to say that two of his deepest friendships were with the two stars whose careers he helped launch, Sandy Duncan and Tommy Tune.

Sandy acknowledged many times that Tom was the mentor to whom she owed her career. She trusted his professional advice completely, confident that he always had her best interest at heart. In 1965, after their successful trip to New York, she wrote to him, "If you told me I was to have a three-week engagement reading poetry at the Dallas YWCA, I would rest assured you had a good reason and that it was for the best!"

Throughout Tom's life, he and Sandy stayed in close contact and saw each other in Los Angeles or New York whenever possible. I met Sandy in 1985 when she was in Dallas for *My One and Only* with Tommy Tune. When Tom and I knocked on her dressing-room door after the show, she took one look at me and screamed, "Oh! You look just like me! I thought you would be a tall, elegant socialite. But you're just like me!"

I laughed, and it was the beginning of a wonderful friendship. Sandy and her husband, Don Correia, have children just a little bit older than our own, and we would all get together whenever we could. We thoroughly enjoyed that family friendship for many years.

Although I had briefly met Tommy Tune when Tom and I went backstage one night at an off-Broadway production, it wasn't until 1985 that I really got to know him. And when he returned in 1987, Kenny and I had the treat of watching him warm up in the rehearsal room. Tommy and Kenny, a toddler at the time, immediately bonded and developed a friendship that continues today.

Tom's publicity portrait, 1992.

"Aunt Patsy" Neumann with Kenny and Ryan, backstage, 1991. Patsy took over the job of Dallas Summer Musicals' wardrobe supervisor from her mother Vivian Faucher, who had worked with Tom for thirty-five years. Patsy managed wardrobe for fifty years before her retirement.

George Stitt, house carpenter, outside the Music Hall with Kenny and Ryan, 1990.
George and Tom not only worked together, but were close personal friends. George was a groomsman in our wedding.

Kenny relaxing at intermission, sitting on Tom's leather sofa in the office, 1990.

Dave Boyd, production property master, outside the Music Hall with Ryan, 1990.

Tom and Ryan walking into the Music Hall for our family's Friday night ritual, 1990.

Tom's office in the basement of the Music Hall was dominated by an intricately carved chair given to Tom by the actor John Davidson and his wife in 1971. The accompanying note read: "Every Pope deserves his throne."

The chair was flanked by two carved lions, a gift from Yul Brynner, from the set of *The King and I*.

Tom in his office, 1987. The "throne," the lions, his collection of canes, the enormous desk, and the solemn tone caused one writer to describe his office as a cross between a 19th-century funeral parlor and a slightly down-in-the-heels club for English gentlemen.

I have loved coming to the office every day since 1955. I find it wonderful, exciting, challenging, just as much now as the first show I produced in 1961. It never loses its wonderment and excitement.

—Tom Hughes

Tom at his desk on a typical day—phone calls, meetings, casting, rehearsals, contracts, schedules, actors, music, sets, costumes, this season, next season, fundraising. He loved every minute of it, juggling it all with dignity and grace.

Tyne Daly (center) starring as Rose in the 1989 State Fair Musicals production of *Gypsy* with Jonathan Hadary and Crista Moore, and with Tom at the opening night party (left).

Stephen Lehew is a Broadway actor who made several appearances at the Dallas Summer Musicals, shown here (right) as Freddy Eynsford-Hill in *My Fair Lady*, 1981. He returned in 1989 to star in *Godspell* and in 1994 for *Seven Brides for Seven Brothers*.

Although Tom didn't usually go out with the performers after the shows, we did go out with Tommy a few times, and it was always wonderful to be with him. He and Tom remained dear friends.

Tom described having Sandy and Tommy on the stage together that summer of 1985 like having the kids home from college—and Dallas audiences certainly responded as if both stars were personal friends. The show set a Music Hall attendance record through sixteen performances, with more sold-out performances than any previous show.

Tommy came back to Dallas Summer Musicals several times through the years. And as a tribute to the man who gave him his start, he gave Tom the cane he had used in his Broadway production of *My One and Only*.

The white-topped, extra-tall black cane was inscribed in lacquered lettering down the side: "For Tom Hughes. Tommy Tune's cane from *My One and Only*. 623 performances at the St. James Theatre on Broadway."

Debbie Reynolds, starring in the 1989 production of *The Unsinkable Molly Brown,* shown here at the opening night party with Tom and the Musicals' longtime supporters Rodger Meier and Barbara Hart Charlton.

Tom with Mayo P. Crum, Jr. and Yvonne Crum at the opening night party for *I Do! I Do!* starring Sandy Duncan, 1992. Mayo and Yvonne were both long-term supporters of the Musicals and served on the Dallas Summer Musicals board of directors and executive committee. Yvonne also served as president of the Dallas Summer Musicals Guild.

Tom with Juliet Prowse, starring in *Mame*, 1990.

Tommy Tune and Ann Reinking in *Bye Bye Birdie*, 1991.
Below, Tom and I with Ann at the opening night party.

The Hughes family, Easter 1993.

I have a wonderful family—a wife and three children.
And I have the theatre.
That's the family.
That's the hobby.
That's the life.

—Tom Hughes

Tom and I typically spent time in Los Angeles and New York each spring for auditions and to see prospective shows. In 1993, however, Tom was preparing the Music Hall for the arrival of the first national tour of *Phantom of the Opera*, elated that he'd been able to secure a long run for Dallas audiences. In addition to overseeing the transformation of the Music Hall for *Phantom*—including installation of the iconic chandelier that hangs over the center orchestra section—he was preparing for the regular season, as well. He was just too busy to leave town. So instead of traveling together, Tom stayed in Dallas, while I took 6-year-old Kenny, 5-year-old Ryan, and 10-month-old Kyle to San Antonio over spring break. Luckily for me, my mother and Juanita Jones came with us.

Juanita had worked for Tom's family as a housekeeper for about ten years before we were married. When our children were born, she began to work for us three days a week as a housekeeper and nanny. Everyone who knew Juanita described her as a saint or an angel. Truly one of the most spiritual people I have ever met, she was a role model for anyone who wanted to live a good and upstanding life. I was always grateful for her presence in our lives, and for the deep love she shared with the children. At our request, Juanita walked down the aisle at Ryan's wedding as grandmother of the bride.

One morning in March 1993, not long after we returned from San Antonio, Tom felt a sharp pain in his right shoulder when he lifted Kyle out of her crib. By the end of the day, he was nearly doubled over in pain. He worked with his chiropractor for the next few weeks, but the pain became even worse. An MRI showed nothing, so the doctor assumed Tom had suf-

fered a severe strain that would eventually heal itself.

The severity of the pain day after day took a terrible toll on Tom. Finally, I insisted he see an orthopedic surgeon, who diagnosed and removed some herniated disc fragments. Tom healed easily from the surgery, but the pain returned almost immediately. He continued to work every day as usual that summer, but he was in constant, agonizing pain.

When the season ended, newly ordered CT scans showed the disc was continuing to deteriorate. The day before our ninth wedding anniversary, Tom underwent a second, and much more serious, surgery. The shoulder pain returned immediately. We were very discouraged.

In mid-October, additional scans showed a small spot on his right lung. The tissue was malignant. Although Tom never smoked around the children or me, he had been a heavy smoker for years and still smoked at work—until that day. He put his cigarettes down, and never picked them up again. Hearing about the spot on his lung shook Tom to his core. I was blessedly naïve, too naïve to be terrified.

Following an extensive surgery to remove the malignancy, Tom developed pneumonia. Those two weeks in the hospital were two of the bleakest, loneliest, and most frightening weeks in either of our lives. But a short time later, we had wonderful news from the doctor. He said Tom was totally cancer-free and had a fabulous prognosis. His physical recovery would still be difficult. But emotionally, we knew we would make it.

We had a momentous night planned for exactly three weeks after this third surgery: Tom was being honored with the Award for Excellence by The Arts Community Alliance (TACA), a major Dallas fine-arts

My Christmas 1993 gift to Tom, a portrait of the children. Kenny, 7, Kyle, 18 months, and Ryan, 5.

support organization. But at three o'clock on the day of the event, he was lying in our bed unshaven and almost too weak to move.

"Groom, can you do this?" I asked him. "How in the world can we get you ready to receive your award in just a few hours?"

He barely had the strength to answer me. But he was determined. "I'll be there, Bride," he said.

And he was. Somehow, we got him into his tuxedo, into a limo, and to the gorgeous ballroom of the Anatole Hotel. It was an extraordinary gala evening with more than 1,000 in attendance. The presentation included a wonderful documentary of Tom's life and a lengthy pre-recorded interview. In that documentary, Tommy Tune described Tom as "the grand seigneur of musical theatre in the country. Not just in Dallas, and not just in Texas, but in the country."

When Tom was finally called up to the stage, the room exploded with applause. It was wonderful to feel the enormous respect, appreciation, and love from the many, many people who had followed Tom's career over the years and had benefited from the world-class musical theatre he had brought to the city he loved.

By the grace of God, Tom made it up the small set of steps to accept the award, and he gave one of the best and most inspiring speeches of his life. His beautiful baritone voice was as strong and dependable as ever. And while I held my breath, he somehow made it back down those steps to our table.

The other award recipient that night was world-celebrated pianist Van Cliburn. As soon as he was introduced, he turned directly to us and said, "Tom, I believe that is the most fabulous speech I've ever heard." Then he delivered his entire remarks directly to Tom, as if the entire evening were nothing more than a discussion between the two of them.

Tom continued to convalesce for many weeks, working on the 1994 season as he was able. He began to improve slightly from the surgery around Christmas, and we had a wonderful time with the children. But in early January, the excruciating pain was back. Eventually, we heard the news no one ever wants to hear: Tom had an aggressive cancer and probably less than six months to live.

As we drove home from the doctor that day, Tom was quiet for a long time. Finally, he spoke.

"Bride, I don't want anyone to know about this," he said. "Let's try to figure this out. Maybe he's wrong."

But the doctor was not wrong. We did everything we could to enjoy the time we had left, and to keep Tom as comfortable as possible, even as he spent those last months in and out of the hospital.

Thursday, April 7, was Kenny's eighth birthday. He made it clear that he would not open any presents until he could go to the hospital to see Daddy. I had a slight cold that day which I did not want to share with Tom, so we went the following night, April 8.

The kids and I arrived at the hospital carrying all Kenny's presents and the leftover birthday cake, and we had a wonderful party. Tom was sitting up in his bed, looking better than I had seen him in weeks, happy and with good energy. Kenny and Tom even built a Lego masterpiece together that night, continuing their long-standing tradition. Later, the kids each took a turn on Daddy's bed, loving and hugging him and telling him good night. He kissed each one and said he would see them soon.

Tom passed away two days later, on Sunday, April 10, 1994.

My favorite picture of Tom, taken in Fair Park when we were out for a walk with the children.

Like any family who loses such a great love, some of those early years were a blur of grief and disbelief. However, with our faith and our friends and community, we managed to move forward.

When Tom and I met, I had been deeply wounded by grief and loss. I had lost a part of myself I thought was gone forever. But his love was a balm that soothed my soul. Tom Hughes healed me.

In return, I hope I was able to help him enjoy the deep, trusting romance he thought he would never find and the family love he had longed for. We had only a brief eleven years together—but any number of years with Tom would have been too few.

Our extended family was always an enormous support, as was the family we created with the staff and crew of the Music Hall, who continued to support us and welcome the children to their backstage home for years after Tom's death. I heard from so many theatre friends whose lives had been impacted by Tom. When Stephen Lehew starred in *Seven Brides for Seven Brothers* in 1994, the program states that he dedicated his performance "to the memory of his early mentor and a true gentleman of the theatre, Mr. Tom Hughes."

Any specific memorial or tribute to Tom would be destined to fall short of the one professional tribute he would most want—the continuation of his beloved musical theatre in Dallas. The fact that Dallas Summer Musicals is well into its eighth decade, shepherded by Tom for so many of those years, is his professional legacy and the best tribute to his work. As past board chair Donald Spies has said, "We are the granddaddy of civic light opera in America, and that's because of Tom."

I believe Tom would also appreciate the beautiful bronze statue commissioned by the board under the guidance of Michael Jenkins. Michael followed Tom as producer and managing director and successfully shepherded the Musicals for the following twenty years. The board chose internationally known Texas sculptor and painter Robert Summers to sculpt the statue of Tom that now graces the Music Hall lobby. It was my pleasure to work with Robert during the process, to make sure the artwork reflected the essence of the man I knew and loved. We needed his three-piece suit and cane to reflect his formal persona and we needed kindness in his face to show his true nature.

"Tom gave his heart and soul and life's work to Dallas Summer Musicals for thirty-three years," I said at the statue's unveiling in August 1996. "This memorial is very traditional. The actual piece itself, the bronze, is extremely strong, yet has a warmth and beauty to it. That's what reminds me of Tom."

Three years later, in 1999, I went to our pastor and close friend, Rev. Dr. Blair R. Monie of Preston Hollow Presbyterian Church, to make an unusual request on behalf of our family. I asked if we could hold a service of remembrance to celebrate Tom's life and legacy on the fifth anniversary of his passing. Blair was extremely supportive. Under his leadership, that service turned a somber time of remembrance into a joyous celebration of Tom's life and the gift of his spirit that continued in our lives.

The sanctuary was filled, the music was glorious, the children shared poetry and Bible verses, and others spoke about Tom. The service was so helpful to our family's journey that we repeated it on the tenth,

I worked with sculptor Robert Summers and his assistant to make sure the artwork would reflect the essence of Tom, best as it could.

Ruth Sharp Altshuler and I at the unveiling of the statue of Tom in the Music Hall lobby, 1996. Ruth and her husband, Dr. Kenneth Altshuler, remained active supporters of Dallas Summer Musicals and our close family friends until her death in 2017.

We are the granddaddy of civic light opera in America.
And that's because of Tom.

—Donald Spies
Dallas Summer Musicals
Chairman of the Board, at the
unveiling of the statue of
Tom Hughes in the lobby of
the Music Hall

Kyle's third birthday, with Juanita Jones, 1995.

fifteenth, and twentieth anniversaries of his death. The format changed somewhat from service to service, but each time, the children would speak in front of friends and family about their father and the gifts they continue to experience through his legacy.

It has been almost twenty-five years since we lost Tom. He would be incredibly proud of his children, now such wonderful adults.

Kenny is a physician, lecturing in pathology at the University of Michigan Medical School in Ann Arbor. Ryan and her husband, Gary Berner, live in Arkansas where she is a pediatric nurse and he is a pediatrician. They are the proud parents of the spectacular Ruby

Alexis Berner, born in 2017. Oh, how Tom would have loved this little granddaughter! And Kyle, the baby Tom used to hold in his arms and serenade, is following her father into musical theatre. A talented singer, dancer, and actress—the proverbial triple threat—Kyle is living in New York City, working her way into the business, like so many of the young hopefuls Tom auditioned.

I, too, have changed my career direction since Tom's death. After staying home to raise our three children, I dusted off my drama degree. Since 1999, I have served as director of fine arts at The Shelton School in Dallas. Whether it's musical theatre or Shakespeare, it is such a privilege to work with these amazing students and share my love of theatre. I hope Tom would be proud.

Tommy Tune has continued to be a wonderful friend to our family, and we see him as often as possible. Just a year or two after Tom's passing, Tommy was in town for a project and called to see if we could meet for dinner. I told him I could, but I also had to attend open house that evening for the children at Parish Episcopal School. No problem, he said, we'll do that, too. And we did.

In 2015, Kyle and I spent a beautiful Christmas Eve with Tommy. We had a wonderful time catching up, and he gave Kyle great advice about breaking into and surviving in the business. Not too long afterward, they ran into each other in the hallway of a rehearsal space in New York—Tommy rehearsing for a show, and Kyle warming up for an audition.

"Uncle Tommy?" Kyle approached him.

"Kyle Hughes!" he yelled and ran over to give her a big hug. "I would know that voice and face anywhere."

Tom would have just loved that.

Idelle Rabin, me, Ryan and Michael Jenkins at the Leon Rabin Awards Announcement Party, 1997. The Leon Rabin Awards honored excellence in Dallas theatre. It was announced that evening that Tom would be honored posthumously for his lifetime achievement in theatre.

Kyle, Kenny, me, and Ryan at the 1997 Leon Rabin Awards.
Tom was posthumously awarded the Standing Ovation Award for his lifetime achievement in theatre.

Tommy Tune with me, Kyle, Ryan, and Kenny, 1997.
He has continued to be a wonderful family friend.

Clockwise from upper right: Kenny, Ryan, Juanita Jones, me, and Kyle, 2004.

Kenny, age 16, with Juanita Jones
at the Music Hall, on their way to see a show.

"Uncle Stuart" Hale, production house carpenter, with Kyle, Ryan, and Kenny, backstage at the Music Hall, 2006.

I always knew Tom had a large influence on a great number of people. But even today, I continue to discover just how far his influence went.

In 2015, when I was helping Kenny move to New York City for his residency program, I decided to visit the famous Triton Gallery to purchase some show posters for my office. I selected several posters to be shipped, and the man behind the counter started some political banter with me about Texas. But as soon as I mentioned Dallas, he became wistful.

"Dallas, Texas. I spent the best summer of my life in Dallas," he said. "I suppose you're too young to know the famous Dallas Summer Musicals producer, Tom Hughes. He was my mentor and changed my life." I introduced myself and asked if he knew Tom had passed away.

"Yes, I knew. I sent you a condolence card!"

When I asked his name and discovered I was speaking to Roger Puckett, we hugged and cried. I had heard his name from Tom many times. Roger told me he had auditioned for Tom and had been cast in the chorus one season when he was a young man. But soon after, he had become ill and had to be sent home. Realizing Roger was devastated, Tom pulled him aside.

"Young man, it's important that you go home and get well," Roger remembers Tom telling him. "But when you recover, you come back to us." That kindness launched a friendship that lasted until Tom died. They often wrote and spoke by phone, and Tom guided Roger's career as he went on to become a successful dancer on Broadway.

In 2017, Dallas Summer Musicals appointed Kenneth T. Novice as president. Although Ken never knew Tom personally, he was well aware of Tom's work. Ken reminded me that Tom was—and still is—known in the theatre world throughout the country.

"Whether I'm here in Dallas, in Los Angeles, or New York, Tom's name is still mentioned as creating high-quality musical theatre for over three decades," Ken says. "Our goal for the future is to continue that wonderful legacy."

During the first summer of Ken's tenure, I attended a Musicals performance with two close friends and my daughters, who were home on a visit. On our way out, we stopped in the lobby to look at the statue of Tom and stood there talking for a bit.

"Let me tell you about this guy," a woman said as she walked up to us.

One night, she had arrived at the Music Hall and purchased a ticket for that night's performance. She then went to dinner at the Old Mill Inn Restaurant, just a short walk from the Music Hall. That's when she realized she had inadvertently purchased a ticket for the wrong night. She went back to the box office to see if they could do anything for her, but she wasn't hopeful; she knew she should have checked the ticket at the box office.

"Well, there was Mr. Hughes standing right there. He told me he was the head usher, and yes, he could definitely help me—and boy, did he!" she recalled. "He not only took back my balcony ticket for the wrong night, but he gave me a fifth-row center ticket for that night at no extra charge. Can you imagine?"

"Actually, I can imagine. That sounds just like Tom," I said. I introduced myself and the girls to her.

"Well, you sure are a lucky family," she said. "He was one fine man."

Yes, he was one fine man. A man who saw the best in others every day of his life.

That was my Tom.

The Hughes family at the Music Hall, 2018.
Gary Berner, Ryan Hughes Berner, Anné Hughes, Ruby Alexis Berner, Kyle Hughes, Kenny Hughes.

Acknowledgments

Tom was always the first to say that a great part of his success in creating the premiere summer theatre in America was his extraordinarily talented, five-star stable of designers and directors, including:

Raymond Allen, music director

Gene Bayliss, director

Toni Beck, choreographer

Michael Biagi, music director

John Bishop, director

Jean Browne, music director

Forrest Carter, director

Eddie Gasper, choreographer

David Gibson, lighting designer

Jack Holmes, music director

Rob Iscove, director/choreographer

Lawrence Kasha, director

Jack Lee, music director

James Leon, music director

Michael Maurer, director

Eivie McGehee, choreographer and house manager

Larry Miller, music director

Gus Schirmer, director

John Sharpe, choreographer

John Tedford, music director

Lucia Victor, director

Sheila Vaughn Walker, music director

Peter Wolf, scenic designer/art director

Randel Wright, stage designer

He also couldn't have done without the backstage and front of house crews that made Dallas Summer Musicals so successful for performers and audiences alike, including:

Adrienne Allen, advertising

Bill Bingham, production electrician

Billy Bingham, production electrician

Virgil Bingham, house electrician

David Boddie, house manager

Jamelyn Boles, executive secretary

Vicki Boston, executive secretary

David Boyd, production property master

David A. Boyd, Jr., production property master

Greg Brown, production assistant

Kit Carson, stage manager

Jay Carvell, office assistant extraordinaire

Hyman Charninsky, orchestra manager

George Cooper, production associate

Cleo Craft, box office manager

Lanham Deal, director of publicity and public relations

Alice Dewey, production stage manager

Kay Ellis, director of public relations

Vivian Faucher, wardrobe supervisor

Audrey Frankowski, stage manager

Joseph Godwin, assistant stage manager

Harold Goldfaden, production stage manager and choreographer

Al Grab, stage manager

Norman Grogan, stage manager

Stuart Hale, production stage manager

David Hansen, production stage manager

Patricia Hyde, production stage manager

Debbie Irvin, box office manager

Deborah Louise Jones, production assistant

D.L. Langley, property production manager

Cathy Maberry, executive secretary

Ruby Magnolia, box office manager

Nancy Marshall, casting and production associate

Charles Meyers, orchestra manager

Gerald Morris, sound engineer

Randall Mulry, production stage carpenter

Patsy Neumann, wardrobe supervisor

John V. Osborne, orchestra manager

Ben Perrin, house manager

H.R. Poindexter, production manager and director

Margaret Rodgers, executive production associate and coproducer

George Roland, assistant stage manager

Mildred Sale, director of public relations

George Shaw, house electrician

George Stitt, master carpenter

Becky McQuistion Surratt, executive secretary

Gary Surratt, executive production associate

Bill Toon, production carpenter and electrician

Philip Vansyckle, stage manager

Joe Watson, assistant stage manager

Nelson Wilson, assistant stage manager

Frances Fazio Winikates, assistant box office manager

To those who worked tirelessly to help this book come to life by providing information, by reading or editing, and to those who provided that one crucial bit of missing information, my heartfelt thanks.

First and foremost, my deepest gratitude to my coauthor, Janis Leibs Dworkis, whose immense talent, heart, and work ethic have made this book possible.

My profound thanks to Sally Saldo Veon, Dallas Summer Musicals' archivist and 1960s performer, and Jean Browne, music conductor and the Jack Lee archivist, whose efforts were crucial to the development of this book.

My deepest appreciation also to Steve Beene, Gary Berner, Ryan Hughes Berner, Yvonne Crum, Jennifer Deaton, Sandy Duncan, Greg Farnsworth, Harold Goldfaden, Laura Gordon, David Hansen, Laurel Hoitsma, Kenny Hughes (for the use of his amazing book about his father), Kyle Hughes, Stephen Lehew, Nancy Marshall, Kathy Martin, Cyndy Monie, Katy Rubarth, Nancy Skochdopole, Suzanne Stell, and Tommy Tune.

Photo Credits

Page	Credit
16	Courtesy, the Dallas Jewish Historical Society, Dallas, Texas
23	Agner International Photos, New York
27	Mack Long
41	Andy Hanson
45	Andy Hanson
47	Clint Grant, *The Dallas Morning News*
53	Clint Grant, *The Dallas Morning News*
54	Andy Hanson
57	Andy Hanson
60	Doris Jacoby Photography
61	Doris Jacoby Photography
66	Friedman-Abeles ©, New York Public Library for the Performing Arts
76	Andy Hanson
78	Smith/Garza Photography
84	Smith/Garza Photography
89	Andy Hanson
90	Smith/Garza Photography
92	Smith/Garza Photography
99	Andy Hanson
113	Andy Hanson
114	Andy Hanson
115	Andy Hanson
116	Ernst Haas
129	Kenn Duncan ©, Billy Rose Theatre Division, NY Public Library for the Performing Arts
131	Kenn Duncan ©, Billy Rose Theatre Division, NY Public Library for the Performing Arts
136 (top)	Andy Hanson
137 (top)	Andy Hanson
140	Milton Hinnant
155	Bill Canada
157	Milton Hinnant
159	Robert C. Ragsdale
163 (bottom)	Andy Hanson
167	John Haynsworth
181	Connie Roper Photography

All other photographs courtesy of the Dallas Summer Musicals Archives, the Jack Lee Archives, and the Tom Hughes Archives.

Bibliography

Allis, Tim. "Arts Musicals Man." *D Magazine*, July 1984.

Anderson, Porter. "The Gentleman Producer." *D Magazine*, June 1992.

Blackwell, M.I. "Marketing the Arts." *The Dallas Morning News*, July 9, 1986.

Bowman, Harry. "What's the Ticket to a Hot Season?" *The Dallas Morning News*, August 13, 1985.

Bowman, Harry. "The Sound of Music for 50 Summers – Dallas shows survive war and June bugs." *The Dallas Morning News*, May 20, 1990.

Crockett, Lane and Reese, Sally. "Music Hall's Tom Hughes, He's Had a Long Love Affair with Dallas Summer Musicals." *Shreveport Journal*, July 26, 1974.

The Dallas Morning News. "360 Audition for Roles in '63 Summer Musicals." May 20, 1963.

The Dallas Morning News. " 'Molly Brown' to launch Musicals." June 9, 1963.

The Dallas Morning News. "Pearl's 'Dolly' Musicals Repeat." January 28, 1975.

DeSanders, Janet. "Tidbits: 25 Years of Summer Musicals." 1976.

Heimberg, Martha. "Rejoice! Dang it! still works, as does Tom Hughes." *Dallas Downtown News*, September 6, 1982.

Hughes, Kenneth. *Tom Hughes*. St. Mark's School of Dallas. Dallas: printed by the author, 2002.

Hughes, Tom. "Tom Hughes: An Oral Interview." Interview by Gerald Saxon, November 22, 1982.

Hulbert, Dan. "Making a Splash: Texas-size 'Rain' opens Summer Musicals." *Dallas Times Herald*, June 6, 1986.

Leydon, Joe. "Galaxy of stars to headline Dallas Summer Musicals." *The Dallas Morning News*, March 26, 1980.

Luker, Carol. "DSM's Hughes tells the feast, famine of musical fare." *Dallas Downtown News*, May 6, 1985.

Mitchell, Sean. "Unique: Tom Hughes, a theatrical manager in the grand old style." *Dallas Times Herald*, February 2, 1983.

Neville, John. "Hepburn Brings Show to Dallas." *The Dallas Morning News*, February 13, 1977.

Neville, John. "The Dallas Musical Scene." *The Dallas Morning News*, May 29, 1977.

Neville, John. "MGM Stars Turn to Stage." *The Dallas Morning News*, June 4, 1978.

North Texas Daily. "Tom Hughes." February 6, 1986.

Payne, William A. "Musicals Pick New Stage Chief." *The Dallas Morning News*, March 1, 1963.

Porter, Bob. "Summer Music Man Arrives." *The Dallas Morning News*, May 15, 1964.

Porter, Bob. "Tom Hughes, Musicals Man." *Dallas Times Herald*, September 10, 1962.

Porter, Bob. "The Summer Musicals: Dallas' Best Foot Forward." *Dallas Times Herald*, July 9, 1978.

Primeau, Marty. "High Profile: Tom Hughes, the cane-toting impresario behind the Summer Musicals is everybody's favorite producer, a role he's relished for almost 30 years." *Dallas Times Herald*, May 19, 1985.

Primeau, Marty. "A Cane for All Seasons." *The Dallas Morning News*, April 19, 1987.

Primeau, Marty. "Three Hours with Tom Hughes." *The Dallas Morning News*, August 23, 1987.

Rosenfield, John. "The Passing Show." *The Dallas Morning News*, August 26, 1947.

Smith, Russell. "Phyllis Diller Can't Keep Up." *The Dallas Morning News*, August 20, 1984.

Weeks, Jerome. " 'The Phantom' will finally swoop into Dallas in March 1993." *The Dallas Morning News*, June 9, 1991.

Werts, Diane. "Neil Simon and Paul Lynde are this summer's odd couple." *The Dallas Morning News*, June 19, 1980.